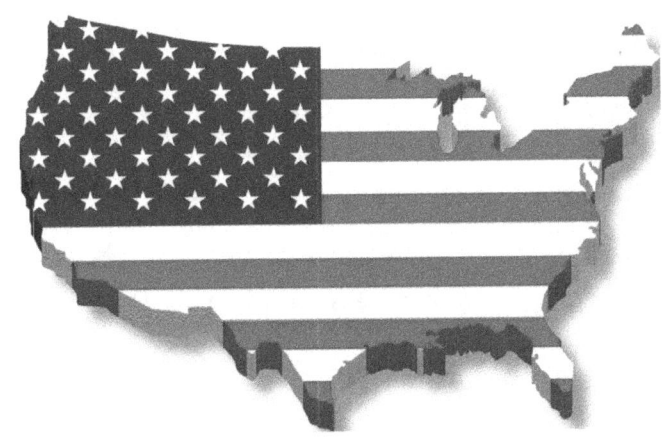

LAND OF OPPORTUNITY

Opportunities and Guarantees in America

And a Sobering Recognition that It Takes Work to Achieve Them

By

Joseph K. Goldstein

By the same author

Things of Concern- *a Dissertation Relating to the State of the World and the State of Mind*

All Things Relate- *a View of the U.S. Economy*

Moments of Impact- *My Personal Inquiry Relating to the Formation of Self*

Two Visions- *Pathways in Nature Artwork*- *(with Donna Jean Goldstein)*

Look At Me- *My Journey through Time and Experience*

ISBN   13: 978-1542681162

ISBN   10: 1542681162

Goldstein, Joseph K.,   1938-
Land of Opportunity/Joseph K. Goldstein- ed.1.1 P. cm.

   1. Sociology-21st century-commentary
   2. Politics-21st century-commentary
   3. Economics-21st century-commentary

"LAND OF OPPORTUNITY"
featuring such trivia as:
WORK, PLAY, IDEAS, LEISURE, HAPPINESS, SECURITY, LOVE, PEACE
And OH SO MUCH MORE

Contents

BY WAY OF INTRODUCTION

Sometimes I just get that itchy finger and need to use the surrogate pen (fingers on keyboard) to put down what is going on inside my head, my mind is so full of thoughts about events in the world and about my personal feelings relating to these trends and occurrences. Mostly, it is about things that bother me deeply, things that have either been entrenched within society for years or that are currently worming their way into various societies and ways of thinking. Over the course of the last 15 years I have written three books and co-authored one art publication, two of the books have world impact themes, and one a personal theme. The topic of this book, material on freedom and free choice, really dovetails with the other three books in presenting choice as the most important underlying parameter of living.

I have to start out by saying that I am probably heavily biased by my life experiences, by the readings and by words that I have heard. I am sure this will come through in what I am saying in this book. But know that what I intend, and what I surely hope for, is that a person perusing this missive will say either Hoorah or dang-it, because then I will know that someone has taken the time to either agree or disagree. And that would be my sole reward, my only desire here; to surface situations, engage the reader and evoke a reaction. Like it or not, suitably stirring up feelings and intellect offers reward itself. I would feel that I have reached out with a result, with a form of feedback that I may never see, but that exists nonetheless.

My writing style seems almost patterned after Hugh Prather who wrote "Notes to Myself" well over 50 years ago, which was a musing and meandering romp through observations of life. I am also looking at life, but with a different perspective, one where interactions within society are the building blocks of our pathway. And one, where looking at current trends, there can be an extrapolation that offers a rather disconcerting world-view: one without major innovation, without incentive to produce, without pride in ability, and with the fear of looking behind you. But guess what, that is only one of myriad possibilities. I see so many wonderful paths forward that I have to shout out that where you head is of your own choice, and that is what prompted me to explore our wonderful country and what our founding fathers tried to build into its structure.

While writing this book, I came to realize that the subject matter is not as easy to present as I thought it would be. My original intent was to demonstrate that the Constitution and Declaration of Independence were much under-appreciated by our citizenry, and that our institutions of learning were falling far short of a goal for appreciation of what our country really is and represents. And as I wrote, I came to the conclusion that in addition to lack of development of appreciation, there was also lack of awareness and lack of depth. I knew most of the basics, but did not have a really perceptive understanding of them. So as I wrote, I had to stop, analyze, appreciate, interpret, and finally place cogent words on paper. Then, when I re-read them, some level of depth began to emerge; nothing popped out, no eureka, just appreciation. And mostly, I have embellished appreciation through presentation of both interpretation and opinion.

Within this missive, I have included some of my thoughts that have often been shared with those willing to listen, and even offered to those who didn't want to hear. As you read, you will see that my basis of viewpoint is one of self-determination and pride. That is what makes our country shine, "go for it and get it", remembering that respect for each other's goals is paramount. Translate your capabilities into a commodity that allows you to live and thrive. Others have done it, and the path is available.

By the way, you will also see four sketches that I have inserted, they were done way before the book. They represent my looks at some areas visited, and are just eye candy for the enjoyment of what this country offers. Maybe no big deal to some, but to me they bring a welcome smile and good memories of what life is all about.

Read and enjoy, *Joe*

THIS IS PART OF PFEIFFER BIG SUR FOREST
It was part of a road trip

WORK ETHIC

I have very strong basic agreements with the way our country was founded. That should not come as a surprise to anyone who looks with pride at achievement; because I grew up in this wonderful country of ours, where opportunity abounds and freedom of choice is our anchor of reason. Moral fiber implies that working hard offers rewards, that the fair trade between applying your body and mind in exchange for remuneration is the thing that runs the great economic engine of American Free Enterprise.

So I am saddened and conflicted when I see that the "entitlement crowd" is trying to receive the support of, and endeavoring to transform, our government for yet another inroad against free choice. For example, the not-to-long-ago issue of the Boeing Aircraft Company's struggle to improve their competitive position by reducing costs through new facilities in a region with reduced overhead and less expensive labor. (I don't even mean overseas, which at this time would be the ultimate move, but I speak of locating in a region where wages are not artificially inflated as a consequence of overzealous co-operative bargaining). I am looking at the cost of living and the corresponding wages for income in areas where unions CAN represent, but are selected by choice, not ukase. This is no small issue, and has many important facets. Unions at one time were the collective voice of essentially vocal-less groups that worked under abominable conditions. Although eventually free enterprise would have allowed the worker to migrate towards better job opportunity, the union represented a shortcut choice. Nowadays, things are significantly different, and entitlements of the current variety, which include unwarranted cost of living increases without increased production capability, significant benefits supplied as overhead, reduced work-times, certain seniority benefits, and oh so many more, are all things that defy the American work ethic. If a person is not satisfied with, or does not feel comfortable with working conditions, then seek out new conditions such as a different job. If the original conditions were excessively onerous, then jobs with those conditions would not be filled at the current wage scale. If the jobs are filled, then the workers are satisfied with both the conditions of employment and the wages received. That is called a contractual agreement between consenting adults; the two parties-the individual worker and the company for which they work.

Take a look at it from the company point of view. The business environment is a condition that a company needs to examine continuously, because after all, the business exists to primarily provide profit to its owners, and secondarily to enrich the community through employment, through profit-related taxes, and other community service. If the environment is negatively contributory, then the company has every right (nay obligation) to review its position and institute improvement. And if a more appropriate, business-friendly environment can be found, and the cost benefit is clear, then NO ONE should interfere with the private enterprise conditions that allow a thoughtful business decision to be made.
Definitely, the government should not be involved, because after all, the only purpose of government is protection of the RIGHTS of its citizens (life, liberty, and the pursuit of happiness), not the establishment of further entitlements and coercions. Seem familiar? See the Declaration of Independence of the United States.

So as you can see, I am personally a product of our wonderful free enterprise system, wherein regulation exists only as a method of assuring freedom by preventing impingement upon citizen's property rights. These rights include the ability to make their own contract and choose where and with whom they will work. Protection of this right was a basis of establishing our government, and the purpose of government should never be bastardized to allow it to burgeon into becoming a monster intending to substitute control of rights for protection of rights. As a corollary, and with the same perspective, is the universal selector, the vending machine, which offers itself and its products to anyone who wants it and satisfies the only ground rule, which is exchange, and that means an employer-employee contract that only looks at the benefit to each, regardless of any other factor.

ON THE SUBJECT OF MINIMUM WAGE

Basically, economics is a very simple subject. Everything affects everything, i.e....all things relate. With that as a working premise, take a look specifically at our free economy and the impact of ukase-established minimum wage increase.

In a free economy, people offer their skills in exchange for a wage which they then use/spend as they see fit to do. This means that if you are entry level or offer unskilled capability, you search until you find either a position that pays acceptably or you develop a stronger skill set that commands your required minimum. That is all well and good, because it speaks to supply and demand, to free choice, and to desire for improvement, each of which are absolutely the by-words of our democratic, capitalist system.

However, decoupling the supply and demand cycle through artificially increasing wages, ("there oughta be a law"....) immediately ripples through the economy. **When the "cost" of goods increases, then the price of goods increases. When the price of goods increases, then the cost of living increases. If the cost of labor has risen without a corresponding increase in productivity, then the value of the dollar is reduced. Very simply, if I pay you more and you don't do any more, then your contribution and worth has not increased and the extra wage I pay you has no real additive value.**

This affects everyone. If a person is on a fixed income, this means everything costs more and therefore the fixed income will get you less. If you are earning an income, then the cost of living has risen and you will need to demand more in order to maintain your current standards. Thus begins the spiral of COLA (cost of living allowance) which gets you more at no improvement in output, and therefore eventually reduces the value of your wage.

Where this has maximum impact is consideration of off-shore competition. The dollar and the worker become less competitive in the world market; and make no mistake, we live in a world economy.

So this simple demand for increased minimum wage can in fact hurt every American.

But there is something that can be done. It has to do with the nature of free market forces, ingenuity, and desire. Reduce waste and non-productivity, bring manufacturing jobs back to our country, cut the non-productive aspects of government laws and spending, and cut entitlements by putting more people into productive labor. These are things our government can support by focusing specifically on what government was chartered to do, which is protection of citizen's rights to "life, liberty and the pursuit of happiness" (sound familiar?), and specifically, to cut regulation and rules, and to cut the bureaucratic staffing that costs us 25% of our economic product. That's right, look it up yourself and be assured. You got it, that's how much government takes from the economy, that's what "life, liberty and the pursuit of happiness" has been given as value. And by cutting some of the non-productive expenses and give-aways, and beginning to focus on improving our competitive nature, we will no longer need to meddle with nature's most potent natural law, that of supply and demand. That is the long term alternative to "there oughta be a law", which solves nothing and only adds to the need for more control.

TO MY PRESIDENT AND MY CONGRESSPERSONS: A PLEA AND AN OFFER
-sent as an open letter-Feb, 2013- to President Obama

I am extremely concerned that there has been a major disconnect between the electorate and the elected, and the appointees of the elected. This starts with fiscal irresponsibility, and continues with rejection of the free enterprise system in favor of a socialistic perspective that is contributing to this fiscal irresponsibility. "Information dis-information" seems to be developing, with not one pure statement that correlates to campaign promises, with a concerted effort on the part of congressional leadership to misinform and run with agendas far above and beyond any clear-cut sensibility.

I hear words, but do not see actions relating to them, I see actions and absolutely no transparency nor prior discussion presented to constituents.

Am I talking in riddles or- without even providing supporting statements, do you understand what I am talking about? The reason I ask this question is that truly this is a test of everyone's integrity. Start out with the purpose of government. It is to protect the right to freedom of the individual. It is a compact made between the electorate and the elected. It is not to create new rights, but simply to function as the collective protectorate of its citizens. Typical of mankind, we have taken the simple and expanded it into the complex. We have moved so far into the miasma of this "government" thing that we have lost sight of the simplicity of the concept.

I look at the standing of our country in the world as we know it today. As a spokesperson for this country, how can you be proud of what the leadership is doing to us as a nation? This is a trend, and that means NOT a party issue, but a political issue, because both parties have been fumbling forward (?) and stumbling badly. It would be my pleasure to speak with you personally and discuss not only my views, but my offerings of solutions. I have a book in publication at this time ("All Things Relate"), which is relevant and timely to so many of our issues that I would gladly make a copy available for your perusal. The choice is yours, just ask and a copy will immediately be on its way to you.

It is not my intent to push a book, but the ideas within it are critical to redirection of our future, because what I project from our current direction is an irreconcilable mess.

Please respond, and I am pleading for response, so that a dialogue can be established with you or any of your appropriate sub-ordinates.

In all sincerity,

Joseph K. Goldstein

AND NEXT: THOUGHTS FOR THE FUTURE

I am a firm believer in capitalism and the free enterprise system. Well, the 2012 and the 2016 elections are now over, the results not particularly to my liking, either one, but we have to march forward and onward. My citizenship and my beliefs still remain anchors in my life, although these elections showed me that what is important to me is not necessarily as important to someone else. Really, that is nothing new, because everyone is a different product of life, and I knew that. What is a surprise is how things of importance are "sooo" amazingly different to different people. And so I will adjust to this recurring political reality and modify my interactions. Somehow, of the messages of the campaign, and of the beliefs of people, although it was almost a 50/50 popular split, the electoral college procedure trumped all that. The system is good, I don't have a problem with it, because the system looks at geographical regions and lumps them with the intent that local thought is paramount, and the sum of local thoughts represents the will of the people. It gives regions a chance to be heard, and lets minority rule come forth somewhat.

I trace the will of the people back to three educational sources, one- the family, two-the school system, and three- life's experiences. My personal beliefs premise that each of us has talents and it is our own responsibility to convert those talents into providing support for our chosen life's path. I look with pride on my own accomplishments, just as does everyone else about their own life. I have the deepest respect for what I consider personal property, which to me consists of a person's life, thoughts and beliefs, and accumulation of physical things. And I feel strongly that everyone should respect such personal belongings and thoughts of others, as well. That is the basis of the laws of this land, what the Declaration of Independence and the Constitution offer as guidelines and baselines for this great land of ours. And so long as these ideals are not violated, I can easily adjust to life's political whims.

We can now see if the re-elected administration (2012) looked at everybody and represented them all, and if it had modified its goals to recognize that it does represent everyone- those that agreed and those that would have chosen another path. That is not an easily achieved goal, because both portions of the equation need some semblance of movement in order to begin the coming together that is so important. I do not feel comfortable with some of the direction. I know that things socialistic continued to pop up and had a strong champion in the newly elected 2012 administration. That is part of my concern , because I see *that* direction as enabling, not creating. Darn it, but the idea of **taking** from someone else to give to another is just not in my genes. It violates my basic principles of standing on your own two feet. (On the other hand, if given by choice, I can applaud that action.)

Well, there obviously was another way to look at it, and that is what was happening. So then, perhaps the intent is to provide a new baseline, one in which certain things are to be considered common, and all the rest are personal. Sounds good, but where is the line drawn? At what point isn't it appropriate to take away without choice? Or really, when is the first time that it is recognized as theft? I am boring down to some of my personal basics: that your property is yours, and if it is taken without your concurrence, it **is** theft.

It remains to be seen what will happen with the new 2016 administration, certainly the history of the new president and the staffing he is assembling offers a change in direction.

SMALL MINDS DO SMALL THINGS DO –an Op-Ed piece during 2012-2016

The biggest thing about "sequestration" is the length of the word, and the smallest thing is that there seemed to be no apparent way to avoid it.

Does that sound backwards? I think not. Let's examine:

Firstly, whatever happened to bi-partisanship? It did not exist. The reason was simple. Ideology had gotten in the way of thinking logically.

Secondly, how come the parties had decided on all-out warfare and entrenchment? This too is simple, and it is that having backed oneself into a corner, there is no escape unless the ground rules change.

Thirdly, why are the positions so extreme that they take precedence over governance of our country by the elected representatives of our people? Because there has been a decoupling of interests, and instead of looking at the country, the interest is in getting elected and supporting a party by not being out of lockstep with its platform.

But equally uncomfortable is what the presidency had done to the country. Here we had an elected officer that was ushered in with very little more than a majority. The office is President of ALL the people of the United States, and must represent all of them. Representing 51% leaves the other 49% out in the proverbial cold. So what is the office about anyway? I thought the occupant was the elected executive of the people and their interests, and is someone who essentially does not follow political party lines, but looks to the constitution to determine the best course for the country. Not a personal agenda, and not considered the leader of a party, but the elected executive speaking for and representing the very best interests of the country.

That is not what I saw, that is not what I have seen in over seven years. I am watching politics at its extreme, the daring-do and gambling with the future that might make sense if we were dealing with a crap-shoot in Las Vegas, but holy moly Batman, not from the Office of the Presidency.

Why am I feeling so sad, so torn, so disheartened? I have narrowed it down to only one main issue, and that is the mind-set and agenda of whoever us our illustrious leader. Instead of looking at the country, there is looking at small groups of people. Of course these groups make up the populace, and the laws that have been in effect for the life of the country to date allow addressing each and every issue. The executive carries out the will of the people, the legislature defines the rules of "engagement", and the judiciary assures that interpretation is appropriate. Once again and with gusto-THE EXECUTIVE branch carries out the will of the citizens. So stop being all things to all people as thou wilt define it, and please take up the banner of keeping this country sound on a financial, safe, and world-interactive basis. Pursue such goals bearing in mind that the Constitution defines the rights to life, liberty, and the pursuit of happiness for each and every citizen, and that it is the requirement and purpose of elected government to protect these citizen rights, not to control and dictate.

And now we have a new administration, almost the antithesis of the old, but the same entreaty applies-use care in establishing paths, because you represent everyone.

ON THE SUBJECT OF UNIFICATION AFTER ELECTION 2012 and into 2016

Looking back from 2009 through 2016:
Whew, we have just been through the wringer and we came out scathed but hopefully intact. It is a sad state of affairs when the elected and appointed government people get so wrapped up in dirty underwear and ideological unrealism that the entire world watches in shock and awe.

Three separate groups need to re-think and re-orient their monkey-minds; these are in no particular order. The DEMOCRATIC PARTY- so absolutely intent on an agenda of entitlement that the basic premises of our country- the right to life, liberty, and the pursuit of happiness, the protection of which and only for which our government was formed, has been twisted in concept of government from citizen protection to citizen nanny. The REPUBLICAN PARTY- a no nonsense agenda focused on fiscal responsibility and reducing the size of government by defining minimal government charter. Certainly commendable, but presented in so skewed a manner that only zealot ideologues can fully embrace it.

PRESIDENT BARACK OBAMA- here is the saddest of all. Over the past 7 years, this man's agenda has presented itself so clearly and in such an ingrained manner, that there can be no doubt as to what internal mechanisms are at work. It started with the concept of income redistribution, which remains a steadfast and baseline goal. And it has finally spouted into vitriolic, his "withering day-after criticism" that the government shutdown was a Republican-provoked spectacle that "encouraged our enemies" around the world, that only his agenda is the high road.

This man was elected to the highest and most respected office in the world, one that lends its respect and authority to the office-holder. But not for this man, because he brings divisiveness to the office and to our country. This is not his country- his country is in his mind, one that he wishes to make, and it is a sad place. No pride in self-accomplishment will be found there, only the concept of "give me because I deserve", only the concept that everyone owes you something.

What will that do, and what is it doing? It reduces the worth of each individual; no longer can you translate your God-given talents into products for your own needs, because of the entitlements that are attacking your worth; and the resultant "taking without effort", the value of each man's labor is significantly reduced. This translates into a reduction in the value of your labor and of the US dollar because value is not received, and the net effect is that the nation is poorer in the world market.

Is there a solution? Of course there is. It starts with an open mind and the concept of compromise, nothing new to the definition of politics, but certainly a lost premise of our current system. The free market system, which says build it and a path will be beaten to your door, is the answer. One real purpose of government is to assure the unimpeded operation of the marketplace, where there are products that cost from low to high, and offer product capability ranging from minimal to maximum. Taking our current donnybrook as an example, health care insurance offered by private enterprise can run from low cost "catastrophic coverage" to high cost "everything coverage". As far as pre-existing conditions, research funded from some of each company profits must be performed to ease the burden and find a cure. And then surprisingly, the companies will also benefit by reduction in pre-existing conditions. Oh my gosh, can we do it? YES WE CAN!!

But no one arrives unscathed after walking through fire. Hillary is still under the onus of untrustworthy, which relates to BS on Benghazi, absolutely a bad call on emails, even such as her senate term from New York. Trump is another story- the guy seemed set on destroying himself and the Republican Party, and he just might help destroy the legacy of the United States at the same time, by essentially pushing people away and into the Democratic or unaffiliated camps. What an election cycle this is turning into- no one wants what's out there. Maybe a third party candidate stands a chance in this one, if the platform makes sense, because there will be shifting from the Democrats, from the Republicans, and from the unaffiliated into that camp.

Well, 2016 election over, and surprise, from the theory of false alternatives that offered the broken-arm or the broken-leg party choices, the broken leg won. So here is opportunity rift, the ability to implement change and perhaps alter direction. But it is essential that the vision go beyond the broken leg choice into one that respects and considers all the people of this great country.   There is a lesson here, and it is two-fold. All the people must recognize that protecting our right to choose our own path is critical, and that our elected officials must get beyond their personal views and use their offices to promote the welfare and opportunities of the people they serve.

IN RESPONSE TO ANTI-WAL-MART DIATRIBE April 2015

It was hard for me to read the article in the Los Angeles Daily News by Tina Dupuy ranting against Wal-Mart. It evoked frustration, guttural feelings of both astonishment and concern, and down-right angst. The article was quite clear in its message: "for those people who are under the auspices of our governmental socialistic support, people (Wal-Mart) should give them even more". In this case, it translates into a demand that Wal-Mart should raise their company minimum salary strictly to supplement a certain group.

Let's look at this very real situation, and try tracing it back to source and thence to solution. Our government and our citizens have recognized that sometimes within the free enterprise cycle, there can be a lack of job opportunity for some, also that there is a class of people truly unable to work to support themselves. Programs have been established to provide subsistence for these groups, and the reality should be that "out-of-work" is a short term condition requiring the individual to seek status wherein they offer their product (which means their capabilities) in exchange for an offered salary. However, those that cannot work, for bona-fide physical, mental, or emotional issues, may require sustainment at the expense of society (a condition derived from charitable roots). Note that these are the only conditions being discussed, the gray areas of "I deserve" are another very moral consideration not to be analyzed at this time.

In discussing unemployment then, we are down to only one group- those short-timers who are not employed, but wish to be so. The job market place is no different than any other arena- a person offers his capability towards fulfilling an open job position- this is called a negotiation. How they match is a function of the two entities, the seller and the buyer. The seller is the potential employee, offering his/her skills to satisfy the needs of the job. The buyer is the employer, who offers a defined position, a defined benefit package, and a posted salary. In the free marketplace, ONLY when the buyer and seller come to terms of agreement does a deal ensue, at that time they become employer and employee. Both parties will have suitably negotiated to ensure mutual satisfaction. If the salary offered is lower than the employee desires, either negotiate or find another position. If someone applies and gets the position, the employer feels comfortable that the offer was sufficient; while if no one takes the position, the offer must be upwardly modified. That is the way free enterprise and the market system work.

Getting back to Ms. Dupuy's rant, when our government (by the way, that means you the taxpayer) subsidizes out-of-work people with food stamps, that is premised to be a temporary condition at best, supplanted as soon as possible with self-sufficiency. In this society or ours, there are different levels of work requiring different level of skills available to everyone, even if it takes training to achieve that level. The decision of any company to put a value on a job is strictly within the auspices of the company, and as I mentioned, if the value is wrong, then a redefinition will occur. After all, the company will need the work to be performed.

So Ms. Dupuy and all your supporting acolytes, you are part of the free market system, and some people enjoy reading your opinions. Others suffer with it, yet we all support your apparent worth by either satisfaction or dis-satisfaction, but certainly no one needs to subsidize your right to write your opinion nor my right to disagree with it. And obviously, you are satisfied with your remuneration because you are still writing, so you too are simply a result of the market forces of the free enterprise system. Thank you very much.

IMMIGRATION LAWS IN ARIZONA-2015

Some people obviously wonder so what, some say unfair, some say whoa. This is an issue for each and every sovereign country, state, territory, and person, to deal with as they will. The issue is simple, it is the word illegal. It means that a representative body is internally in agreement that certain limits exist and cannot be overstepped. In this case, they are the rules for the granting of citizenship. Maybe you personally don't like these limits, and through due process the limits can be changed. In a majority rule situation, that may be all it takes, but whatever the process, there needs to be one. I think it is inappropriate to hold a gun to someone's head and say "gimme".

That is the case when a citizen's tax dollars are appropriated for uses not sanctioned, when illegal means have been used to create status and condition, when "fairness" is a euphemism for let me take from you what I want. This applies to privileges and services, including law enforcement. So long as the word illegal is validly applied to a person's status, there is just cause for questioning the use of taxpayer dollars to support anything but the removal of that illegitimacy. And that means removal of the cause of that status, either through policy change, or through enforcement of the rules of that policy.

In the case of Arizona, the legitimacy of their laws lies within the definition of "States Rights" so long as they are not in opposition to any federal law over-riding them. Clearly the federal government is mired down in the politics of non-offensiveness and political appeasement, to the detriment of every citizen of this country. Also clearly, Arizona is carefully considering the interests of Arizona and the burgeoning issues with a growing illegal immigrant population. So a very simple criterion has been established-are you a US citizen and/or have you legal sanction to be here? If not, surprise, you should not be here until this shortfall is removed.

Equally to the point, the LA City Council has voted in a moral judgment against Arizona's perfectly legal right to govern their own fate, and this is well beyond the fiscal responsibility for which the council members were elected. I do not need someone to tell me what I am to personally support and to say that I, as one of the Angelenos within city jurisdiction, am in concurrence with their opinion. I feel the Council has way overstepped its authority by shifting from fiscally competent (which by the way is not the least bit obvious from their past performance), to moral espousal with detrimental fiscal results. It is precisely because 49% of the people may not agree that the limits of authority of the council are deliberately associated strictly with the fiscal aspect.

It is a testimony to our country that people are literally "dying to get in". However, it is also a major burden to find that such, entering without sanction, end up creating an entire subculture that lives outside and beyond the law of the land. It is not acceptable, it flaunts the very standards upon which the country is based, and citizenry supporting the acceptability of "illegals" are putting other agendas before the valid one in contention, which is strictly "law of the land". Transition is the key to a suitable solution. The fact that illegal aliens were not all immediately removed allowed that many established lives and presence here. That means that the US is culpable to a degree. And in keeping with the concept of smooth transition being the right way to manage change, then I see that the US has to develop a transition-out plan. This means stopping further illegal entry, removing either the stigma of illegality or the removal of such illegals, as well as a retribution/punitive schemology for those who will have the stigma eventually removed.

Teddy Roosevelt, in 1907, offered some thoughts on immigration, which are poignant in that they really do define the mind-set which is welcomed in this wonderful country of ours, a mind-set that says it is a land of opportunity not found in most other places in the world; here is the gist of it, which is easily embraced because it summarizes the desire to be in America.

"In the first place, we should insist that if the immigrant who comes here in good faith becomes an American and assimilates himself to us, he shall be treated on an exact equality with everyone else, for it is an outrage to discriminate against any such man because of creed, or birthplace, or origin. But this is predicated upon the person's becoming in every facet an American, and nothing but an American...There can be no divided allegiance here. Any man who says he is an American, but something else also, isn't an American at all. We have room for but one flag, the American flag... We have room for but one language here, and that is the English language. And we have room for but one sole loyalty and that is a loyalty to the American people."

Hey, this is a complex reality, and unless and until the Federal Government gets its act together, Arizona states-rights are an acceptable way to deal with their own local problems.

MORRO BAY, boats, a neat café, campground- FUN

"A NATION STRIVING FOR EQUALITY"- written in 2015

There has been a lot of talk about equality, but notice the segue from the constitutional equality of opportunity to the focus on income equality. That has become a rallying point for the Democratic Party and its titular figurehead, Barack Obama. Therein lie two of the biggest issues within this country: the first being the individual right to translate your worth into whatever you wish, the second being the concept of demand versus desire.

There is no such thing as a national objective, there is no over-riding and governing entity called the state, there really are only people, joined together in common cause through the government of our country to obtain and retain the rights to life, liberty and pursuit of happiness. All that is required is that the state offer protection to assure that these rights are available to all citizens. Carefully worded and crafted agendas have tried to move these basic agreement goals from what they were to a social system modification that takes from those who have earned things with their own efforts and gives to others who would desire it. Harsh words, and unfortunately quite fitting in some degree. But the right plan is one wherein those who have can invest to continue achievement, and that investment would wisely use the talents of those who have ability by funding their move to constructive output.

A key parameter in this whole discussion is the wealth of the state. The state does not create wealth, does not create product, it offers services. In order to be funded, the monetary source comes from its citizens, obtained either as tax or fee. That is it, and that is all. So be aware that "income equality" in one form consists of taking through taxation or fee, and giving through dole. But really, the concept of income equality comes in two forms, one being redistribution as above, the second being the individual's effort to improve and obtain through translation of effort into reward.

When talking about equality, take a look at the capabilities inherent in the newborn and developed over a life-time. Not everyone has the same intrinsic capabilities, (note that I do not say the same intrinsic worth), some of us can carry a tune, some of us can lift 300 pounds, and yet some of us cannot. But each of us can do with and develop what we have, and that is the equality of opportunity offered in this country, that you can develop your abilities to as far as you can, and then offer them in exchange for value received.

I have no objection to giving, this is a process of choice, wherein a person makes a decision that his life value is improved by offering, and his reward is established by his own codicils applied to the giving. What I object to is taking, and that is what taxation and fees are all about. If there is complete agreement on this taking, then that is fine, and going back to the Declaration of Independence-government is to provide the services that assure life, liberty, and the pursuit of individual happiness. So stop there. The mentality that requires state fiat to grab what they want and apply it as desired without the approval of the giver, that is a danger that corrupts work ethic and individual worth. Don't forget, that if 51% say yes and 49% do not, then that 49% is being forced into compliance.

The idea of minimum wage as a requirement established by the state is another major issue. The free market place offers pay for work, it offers wage commensurate with what the market will bear. So if the consumer wants a product, but the cost + profit of supplying it is excessive, then the consumer looks elsewhere. What this is saying is two-fold. First, to be in business, you must produce at an affordable and competitive price. Second, any arbitrary increase in salary by one part of the economy reduces the value of your own work unless you have had the increase as well. This is like COLA (cost of living adjustment), where each rise in wage is not related to increased productivity, but simply to ukase. The value of the currency therefore is reduced, because for the same output, you are given more wage. So in a competitive marketplace, the guy that charges more because his expenses are higher will lose out to the less expensive, and the net effect of the un-earned increase is eventual loss of competitiveness. The reality is that if you don't like what you do because it doesn't offer enough compensation, then change jobs, improve your skills, and move either up your ladder or into another arena.

Between this newly fashioned goal of touted income equality and the decoupling effect of the minimum wage process, this wonderful country of ours is beginning to see a major downward spiral in enthusiasm and worth. I for one am very unhappy with the prognostication, and unless people recognize this trend and re-establish the basic tenets upon which this country was founded, we will continue down a slippery and terrible slope. The solution? Read the Declaration of Independence, read the Constitution, reaffirm their goals, and salute the American spirit.

HEALTHCARE 102

How do I feel about health? VERY IMPORTANT! How do I feel about Health Insurance? Optional, but silly not to have! Now ask the imbedded question, how do I feel about ACA (the Affordable Healthcare Act- ObamaCare)? That opens conundrums galore, because instead of choice, all of a sudden it becomes ukase, and by the Federal Government, our duly elected reps to assure the blessings of citizens life, liberty, and pursuit of happiness through the auspices of law of the land taxation which has plurality support, but not as high as one would hope for. It's the case of going around and asking if it's OK to take from someone else and getting the nod for sure why not. **But more, because the premise of this great land is that if someone wants to help others, that's up to them.** It gets into the concept of private property and how each person wants to translate their labor from wage into commodity. The issue of expense requires careful examination because free and private enterprise means competition, and that should produce options for least price and value received. Nowadays, the cost of health care goes way beyond simply paying a doctor; forms to fill out mean people or machines to interrogate the data of the form, it means consideration of false claims for care, it means recognition of rights to sue if care is inappropriate, and more. All of this is cost of doing business, and only the weeding performed by competition can draw this cost down to a minimum. Then individuals can look at their needs and the costs of assuring they are met, and look at their priorities and determine what they really require.

Delve a little bit further into this subject, and specifically into the process of healthcare in the United States and see that costs are very high. Whether the bill is sent to an individual or to the government, the cost of healthcare is rightly seen as outside the reach of some, and for that reason, government has stepped in with its mighty hand and grabbed from everybody to help cover the high costs. Did you notice that the issue I am discussing is HIGH COST, because using the concept of insurance, there should be a way to structure cost and service so that everyone gets what they absolutely need. Paying for healthcare takes several forms- one is insurance payments of whatever scope a person sees as necessary, another is to simply pay as you go, and third is to ask or tell someone else to pay for you. Well, you know what I think of the third option, the first and second are the ones for detailed focus. The goal is the reduction of the cost of healthcare. This includes cost of medicines, cost of personnel, and cost of the supporting system to assure facility and equipment availability.

So why is the cost so high that the only way to provide care is to grab from others? It needn't be this way. Let's break it down. Firstly, only get what you need and only when you need it. To have that happen, limited insurance selected by the individual for both normal care and catastrophic care must be made available, with statistical support for cost. Second, staffing of hospitals, medical offices, and care-givers must be carefully selected to prevent redundancy. Thirdly, cost of medicine must be carefully examined to prevent subsidizing extraneous aspects (by this I mean that breakthroughs in research must not be forced to subsidize dead-ends). This is not easy, by the way, because free enterprise and competition always stove-pipes research. But the plan could be to use entrepreneur-ship to gamble or invest in the research and require that adequate presentation material offer the entrepreneur a wise decision matrix to allow that promising studies will be financed. This takes the onus off the research agency and places it into the common realm of private investment. In the case of pre-existing conditions, the cost of care must be borne through the insurance plan but some portion of the cost must be placed into research to assure that such conditions are subsequently eliminated. That would offer the benefit that high costs will be eliminated with time.

AND TERRORISM

How can we not recognize that terrorism has come to the forefront of our thinking, our acting, our socializing, our very way of life? I wrote a book a while ago started after 9/11, taking many years to complete, which presented my realizations about what terrorism represented to the world, how it would affect us all, and what to do about it. All my worst predictions have come forward, and worst of all, everything I discussed is still relevant, even more so today. So I would refer you to that book, "Things of Concern" and tell you it is a pithy read, and what I present here is further thoughts on the subject. First and foremost is my deepest concern that the current administration (today is 12/16/2015) is totally naïve in their foreign and domestic policies. The apparent foreign policy goal is to minimize the firmness in the voice of our country in our affairs with other countries, to steer a follower and bumbling path along the way, to prevent conflicting opinions where they should be voiced, to pontificate rather than act, and to withdraw support from tried and true allies. The result has been the standard law of nature- the vacuum is filling rapidly. The issue-the Declaration of Independence and the Constitutional guarantee for government to protect the life, liberty, and pursuit of happiness of the citizenry. What has occurred is growth of zealot forces that are rapidly consolidating their power base and membership, and expanding their militant influence to the point where our country is now directly affected. Where prior to this time, there was valid concern of Mid-East destabilization, we now additionally have potential infiltration and radicalization within this country.

Obviously, diplomacy would be a preferable method of resolution, not caving in to opposition, but holding forth our positions regarding our national requirements for safety and prevention of realized threats to our stability and life. But humankind, being evolved from lower forms of life, still retains some of the baser instincts, such as the need to exhibit force if necessary to support our positions. However, in some instances, the basic premises of life are different in different areas. Zealots over-ride the desire for life with a religious axiom that anything different is not only a threat, but is an enemy to be destroyed. This is in direct conflict with the premise that property belonging to someone else belongs to someone else and cannot be taken or destroyed. I define property as your life, your physical belongings, and your intellectual rights. So when there is an avowed movement to kill, to destroy, and to eliminate others ideas, it is a threat which must be countered.

Addendum: It is now February, 2017, and our newly elected president has been issuing executive orders. One is germane to this discussion, the temporary hold on immigration from certain areas. The hold is to allow for a new system of assuring that entrants come in good will, and the areas selected are countries known to harbor terrorists. The issue now is that the initial implementation is without sufficient guidelines to focus on the reason for this order. Rightly so, the courts are concerned about rampant overzealousness in implementation. That is all good, because the various branches of government need the checks and balances.

ON SELECTION AND ELECTION OF THE CHIEF

At no time has the process of the presidential election been so upsetting as the 2016 election. Three factors have made this a veritable mess- the primary process, the electoral college, and personalities of the candidates. The electorate is appalled and polarized, and thoroughly disgusted that the United States political process has allowed these two extremely flawed candidates to be essentially the only choices available, with a guaranty that one of them will be governing and guiding this country at least for the next four years unless they do something totally offensive to the point of requiring impeachment.

THE PRIMARY PROCESS:
Seemed like a great idea to allow any party candidate the opportunity to represent the party as the election candidate. It would seem that the party would have sufficient knowledge of the potential candidate and be willing to allow that their endorsement would follow selection. However, as shown in the past when Sarah Palin was selected as vice-presidential candidate by John Mc Cain, and subsequently shown to have been totally improperly vetted in qualifications, it would seem that a governing party committee would look carefully at the potential candidates that would associate with their name and platform, and determine if such candidate met acceptable criteria. The specifics of the 2016 race show massive flaws in both the Democratic and the Republican parties process, both of which allowed laissez-faire to govern their processes, thus meaning that nothing governed their process but fate itself.
In the case of the Democratic Party, there was a contest between an outright socialist who would have completely modified the concept of government of the country; versus a political insider who exhibited not only flawed judgement in decisions, not only flaunting of the classified system designed to protect the workings of the country, but also crossed the line between the authority of the office and personal goals.
In the case of the Republican Party, having allowed 17 primary candidates to vie for favor allowed a very small minority of the party to select a candidate that did not reflect the platform of the party.

Additionally, the personality and selected approach of the candidate placed extreme prejudice as a priority of the message. Thus the party's candidacy was hijacked by the process.

THE 2016 ELECTION AND ITS AFTERMATH:
Well, today is December 16, 2016, the election is supposedly over, the votes tallied and counted, the unification of the country supposedly in process. But I do not see that happening. You may consider that the election legally and procedurally produced a president-elect, and although this is true, the electorate in this election can hardly handle that. In fact, there is such entrenched hard-core volatility, that there is refusal to accept that the citizenry has spoken within the existing rules of the game and that it is truly time to see the bigger picture that the next four years will have an administration commensurate with the election results. It has happened before, it will happen again. The 2008 election and the 2012 election are cases in point; acceptance of the results of the election and of the consequent 8 years of the bent of the party. This election was different, the candidates flawed, the rhetoric visceral, the platforms diametrically opposed, and the many of the electorate befuddled by the theory of false alternatives-"what do you want, the broken-leg party or the broken-arm party", and the ensuing conundrum of poor choices.
So by the time this manuscript is published, all issues will at least be bundled into a solution of sorts, but here are the underlying aspects that remain visceral:
- Personality- does a political neophyte have the necessary awareness to act as the spokesperson for this nation, especially with regard to foreign affairs
- Cabinet- will cabinet members largely gathered from industry be able to handle all necessary aspects of a political appointee office
- Election Tactics- can the release of internet and private correspondence and the intimation that foreign governments supported such, be resolved in a satisfactory manner, and will it have impact on electoral college voting decisions

- Election Process- can the electoral college vs the popular vote be put into the future disposition phase to allow our legal paths to create any desired change.
- Can the extreme visceral impact of dedicated acolytes be quelled to allow for continuance of the normal process of healing a defensive opposition.
- Can a business person use that acumen to truly step up to the shoes he wishes to fill.

I have faith that rational people would resolve these areas in a rational manner, but I do not have complete faith that either the winners or the losers are all truly rational.

ON 2016 -written during Jan 13-20, 2017

One of our wonderful democratic features is the election process. It follows set rules, although the candidates can in fact go as berserk as they wish during the politicking cycle. It is also a wonderful aspect that the results, though sometimes challenged, are done so on a count basis. However, what a mess this election cycle has been. Whittling down on the Republican side from 17 to 1, and that process in itself had created the ability of one candidate to sweep the field, a political neophyte who touted **that** specific qualification as a rite of passage. It neutered the entire Republican Party. And on the Democratic side, one loving favorite and one upstart became the only choices, and eventually left a flawed standard bearer as candidate. So this election was truly an example of the theory of false alternatives, all the way along from the primaries into the actual election. And our choices became the "broken arm party" or the "broken leg party", which would you rather have, and we seethed as we elected one of them.

Now that the election is decided, there is so much animosity remaining that the losing side is close to violence and out-of-bounds emotional distress, and no one is pulling together to salvage the transition out of this miasma. I write this on January 13, 2017, before the swearing in ceremony, and I have fears that ill will is rampant and trying to create havoc. I hope not, I hope that rule of law will trump violence. Just a few days will show us what kind of citizenry we have.

I personally feel that we need to give the elected a chance to show what capability exists, now that the decision has been made. Accept it, support it, let the new administration generate its plans for the future of this great country, and let's see if a new paradigm has any chance of success. Frankly, it seems a mixed bag. The issues are so deeply entrenched that nothing is obvious, and in a way, that is what started this stomach churning.

It starts with illegal immigration; and here's one that has political and moral dimensions. All countries are sovereign, so border control is up to the country to establish in terms of boundary and law. Citizenship is up to the country to determine and approve, and method of legal entry as well. That is what the law of the land is all about. However, there is a definite moral component as well, and that relates to enforcement. If persons have been allowed to stay or have been overlooked, or deliberately not dealt with according to law, then this laxity must be recognized and factored into long term decision-making. If a life-history is generated here, then this must become a big factor in how to deal with such cases. So a multi-pronged approach must be taken; recognizing law-abidingness, duration, family conditions, economic status. The factor of laxity in enforcement has placed an onus on our government, we have to live with and deal with it. Make the laws, enforce the laws, interpret them according to their intent.

Next we have foreign relations and diplomacy. Our country has been a leader in thought and world relations. Our last administration could not handle leading in a forthright manner, and abdicated responsibility by claiming that the US is just another country among "equals". Well, not so, because there is a spectrum within the world community that relates to neophyte, to economics, to trade, to ideology. And the United Nations recognizes that, in the permanent membership of the Security Council. Unfortunately the general assembly of that august body has deteriorated in its resolve to deal with world issues, and has allowed nationalism and ideological agendas to triumph. There is an old saying that "nature abhors a vacuum", and that has been evidenced by the abdication of our last administration and the growing issues and tensions that have filled that vacuum with other players. This in turn leads to discussion of goals of society, and these in turn lead to the nationalistic bent of many of these countries.

Of course there is the economic side of any country. There has been an obvious global trend towards what would make sense in a world-view, and that is that open economic borders will promote wealth everywhere. In the longest of time-frames, this is valid, because pendulums swing and level things positively. Countries with lower standards and costs of living offer cheap labor and so manufacturing gravitates to that end. As time results in pumping more finances into such an economy, the standard and therefore cost of living will rise and level things out. BUT one of the things that I have seen is that transition is the key to change, and how that is handled is critical to well-being. The transition within the US has not been favorable, companies sought out the least expensive alternatives and our country's government did not truly acknowledge the impact here. So rapidly, manufacturing jobs went away, because although automation also impacted things, the moves to offshore were devastating in impact. Well, a more business oriented administration might very well relook the current trends and institute a recovery plan. So long as that truly recognizes a smooth transitional aspect, then with time, the old pendulum will re-swing in a positive vein. Energy policy is another factor, because energy is a world-wide commodity. Again, transition is key to implementation. Balancing energy sources against world and environmental impact is a necessity, because the wealth of resources will control and dominate relations between countries. The need for energy independence is clear, the threat of control of energy imposes a tremendous reality on our dealings with other nations. Balance is essential, and time frame from immediate to transition to final solution needs to be recognized and utilized in thinking.

Well, part of the election cycle was also personality, as politics always is. Neither candidate offered good personality characteristics, and that is also a large issue at this time. The real question is- now that the election is over, can the president-elect gravitate into the institutional position of head-of-country, commander-in-chief, representative of the people, and chief of the executive branch, and drop the persona that has stood him in such good stead over his 70 years of life, and place him as spokesperson of the country? Roughly 50% of the votes said yes, it remains to be seen if his personality can sustain the bigger shoes that must be filled.

AN INTERESTING THING HAPPENED ON THE WAY...

When you look around and see how things are, relative to say 40 years ago, there are some non- surprising differences- socially, politically, and in the workplace. They relate to the globalization that has taken place, albeit what started out as a most wonderful synergy has morphed somewhat. Now, due to the internet, mistrust, and open extremism, the universally global business community has become somewhat lessened in its all-encompassing role. But also, take a look at what is happening here in the US.

Those who have come here looking, and many times illegally, so far most often bring non-technological skill sets to the workplace. (There is a move afoot to better 'vette the legal immigrant to insure capability to contribute through skill rather than just brawn, but not much can be done with the illegal entrant except challenge on the street, which in many areas is hardly legal). And competition in the world market is based on cheaper production, only time will result in the ensuing monetary influx into those economies, producing a higher standard of living and therefore an increase in cost of production. So, for the illegal status in the US, that means that in addition to illegality many offer strictly manual labor as their product. Surprising result (?) is that now there is advocacy to take from those who have the higher level skill sets and essentially tax them through a slowly growing government requirement to support the "others". First note that now there is a different kind of separation, where once it was that people needed to improve their earning capacity, now there are "have and have-nots", it just swung from economics to morality, because "them-thar" have-nots just need something that the "haves" have. This translates into forms of income redistribution to offer welfare status and payment, food, shelter (in other words subsidy), to people who flaunted the law of the land by coming here illegally and then having advocate support trying to praise them with subsidy. Everybody wants to do better, the trick is to do it within the governing system of legality. Each outpouring of taxed subsidy lessens affluence of those taxed (isn't that obvious)??

Politically, the outcry of unfairness resonates with those who are crying; and political parties, being entities that must corral supporters, have divided into two camps- those supporting subsidy and those supporting personal property rights to keep what you have and spend it as you see fit. I have couched this whole discussion in these terms, recognizing that there are major nuances to it. I elect to focus on the biggest issue as I see it, the affront on personal property, one of the basic protected premises of the Constitution. Most economics centers on the concept of property- the physical nature of homes, autos, toys, etc., and a most important category, intellectual property, which is your thoughts, your words, your ideas. To attack this basic right of protection of property hits at the very basis of the foundation of our country.

So here we are now, in an interesting transition stage, with a challenge to the very nature of our country's foundation. Oh woe, what to do? Well, there is a lot that can be done, and it all starts with re-affirmation of the Constitution. But before I launch into that series of steps, I wanted to look at what this country really offers to its citizens, what a wonderful place it is in which to live, to raise children, to love, to enjoy, to relish. And so I shall.

THE WONDER OF IT

Well, my introduction was a combination of many of my opinions put down on paper over a period of years, it basically was my personal dialogue with myself transferred into statements to the world. I summarize that mind-set by stating that I love my country and all it stands for, and I darn well will vocalize to support that position.

For me, America is truly the land of opportunity, in all areas, including work, play, ideas, leisure, happiness, security, communication, what else?? Basically, rights are not curtailed, unless there is a threat that affects the freedoms of or offers harm to the general or even specific citizenry. This follows the guidelines of the Constitution, stating that government functions to protect the rights of its citizenry to life, liberty, and the pursuit of happiness, and that is all. Obviously, the generic nature of the wording is subject to interpretation, and that is where the zealots from both sides like to preen and posture. And, over many years of trial and tribulation, there has been a creeping trend that has crossed the purity of the line, based on power politics, based on the latest concepts and ideas of morality, and based on ideological principle. This is nothing new in the development of mankind, always trying to improve and codify the thought process, always forgetting about Occam's Razor which offers that simplicity is the most efficient use (in this case) of policy, procedure and implementation. And continuously, as the grandiose nature of improvement shines in the mind, just "one more word, one more thing" would surely make it clearer and better. Well, it's really more than that, because in the Yin-Yang of things, there are sides to all realities, many diametrically opposed to each other, and all workable but not with the same goals and ends in mind.

The wonder of it all is that our society is open to change, and as in the free market, there are swings that ping pong us back and forth between the poles of origin. People listen, and then make up their minds, but the problem is absorbing the content, not just hearing it- and then to think critically about issues and decide for yourself the consequences of the path. That is part of democracy, an obligation to make your voice heard in a meaningful way. Is there a right and wrong? Not so obvious, because the underlying premises are essential to the judgement. However, there is a root question which always puts things into perspective, and that is the universal can opener-"WHOSE PROPERTY IS IT?" What that means is that you can do what you want so long as you don't affect the property of others without their consent. That doesn't mean majority rule, it means if it is someone else's, this is an acknowledgement that it does not belong to you, or to your friends, or to half the people. Unless you as the property owner agree to the shift in control, then it is immoral, even if it becomes legal as law of the land. When you are a citizen, you have agreed to certain basic tenets of the society, and if the law is established legally, and you don't like it, you have to use legal means to change it. That is a wonderful thing, because it does give you a direction and a response capability. It also establishes order rather than chaos. Oh, the blessings of freedom!

But this gets right back to a premise that "security is the lowest form of human happiness", which translates into that if you are lazy and don't bother to defend your rights, then you are going to be subjected to the consequences. The law of cause and effect just keeps on operating. So you just don't get something for nothing, and you are the lesser for allowing other's things to steamroll over you. This doesn't mean outright rebellion, it means pushing back, it means resistance to stifling tendencies.

Where this is coming from is that our wonderful country remains so only because we care to uphold its basic premises, but if we don't take care, things will slowly but surely erode and develop into major change. On a happier note, the rest of this treatise will be dedicated to the wonders of our nation, based on the simple statements of the Constitution that offers our citizens the right of protection of "life, liberty, and the pursuit of happiness".

However, there is more to consider, and in this case it means opening the mind to basic foundations of living, basic foundations upon which a country and a society are founded. I have started this discussion by zeroing in on the US Constitution, because in the United States the rule of law is primary, and going in concert with that the law, through the Constitution, guarantees everything else. And the law looks completely open-mindedly at all citizens, offering the ability to be whosoever or whatsoever they wish. This is not necessarily so in many other countries throughout the world, where for example, religion is an integral part of the governing process, thus obviating the conflicts that could arise for resolution, and assuring that there is no conflict, only resolution. In some cases, the sanctity of life is disregarded in support of other doctrine. Here is the crux of conflict, the butting of heads over the basic premises of living.

VISIT TO SEATTLE-flew up for a visit to see our daughter

THE CONSTITUTION

Where to begin in this documentary of the wonders of our country and our society? I think going back in history to a simple summary of the pillars of foundation. Each and every item has its own history, its own reason for being. As I think about the content for this section, I realize that the Constitution of the United States really contains all the essentials, especially within the "Bill of Rights", but the infinite detail and myriad viewpoints of interpretation are what need to be discussed. Because in this wonderful land of ours, our rights are documented and enforced, and the law of the land insures that injustices be reviewed, carefully examined for applicability, and then justly concluded through jurisprudence. The penalties/consequences of effrontery are delineated up front, so there is no question that cause and effect can be well understood.
But this is not so much about the penalties of violation as it is about the basic guarantees of the freedoms presented in the first 10 amendments to the Constitution of the United States, and selected other amendments. Each of the following chapters looks at these wonderful rights.

Bear in mind that significant legal opinion and extensive expansion associated with interpretation of the following already exists, and I am not using these as guidelines for my discussions here. Rather, my perspective is looking at these United States as a place of law and order, a place of freedom of choice, with the only constraints being self-imposed and being those necessary to operate a free society that protects the rights of its citizens to offer the blessings of life, liberty and pursuit of happiness, so long as actions do not infringe on the property of others.

To me, the key is the concept of property. How is it defined, and how do you deal with it. I believe the entire Constitution can be suitably framed around this concept. First-definition of property is paramount to its understanding. I borrow from an august teacher, Andrew Galombos, and use his definition: Property is a volitional being's life and all non-procreative derivatives thereof: thus being anything at all. That means you and yours; physically, mentally, ideologically, whether part of you or owned and purchased goods- all being creations of individual action. This is a breakthrough because it defines intellectual property as your innovations, your actions, beliefs, and intellectuality- orders of magnitude more encompassing than what a patent can provide, than what a dollar can buy. By the way, if you missed it, your word is your property as well.

With this as a definition, then the antithesis is seen as slavery, the control of or seizing of another's property without his consent. A thief enslaves by causing you to give him your service..ie...property, even if he shares what he steals with someone else. Note the correlation to taxation. And coercion becomes the attempted and intentional interference with another's property. Note the correlation to terrorism. And so with such basics in the arsenal, let's examine the Bill of Rights.

AMENDMENT 1 (Speech)

"Congress shall make no law respecting an establishment of religion, or prohibiting the free exercise thereof: or abridging the freedom of speech, or of the press, or the right of the people peaceably to assemble, and to petition the Government for redress of grievances."

So what is all this about?
- LAW
- RELIGION
- SPEECH
- DISSEMINATION OF INFORMATION
- RIGHT OF ASSEMBLY
- RECOURSE

This is one of the biggest of all ground rules for this country, it offers that after government is formed, it must not get in the way of what you believe and the ability to so say. It is surely a foundation for freedom. So when it comes to beliefs, like whatever religion, so long as you don't impose on others, then this country will accept how you act, how you speak, how you portray yourself. The government will stay out of the way, it will not proselytize, it will not dun, its recognition is in the fact that it will leave you alone. Not necessarily so with how individual citizens will view you, because then you are exposed to ego, opinion, and dispositions. In this case, it comes down to respect for intellectual property, which is what your beliefs are based on.

Look carefully around the world and see how many countries offer all the goodies that are available here. Property is the key, property being defined as your physical ownership and your intellectual acumen as well. Taxation and fees are the passwords out of protection of property so long as you freely subscribe, and the balance between subscription and theft is always on a tightrope.

When our government was formed, it was on the premise that its only purpose was protection of and for citizen's rights to life, liberty, and the freedom to pursue happiness. The first amendment takes the basic ground rule and begins the process of defining what, how, and why. The right to beliefs, communication, and challenge are built into it, as well as teeth through due process of law.

Read and understand the amendment text. "No law respecting an establishment of religion" has two contexts; one recognizing any established religion and that no law may constrain or enhance it so long as it does not interfere with the rights of others, the other allowing that any religion may be established. Hands off is the word, non-judgmental-ism the method. So any person in these United States has the right to believe as they wish, to do anything that they wish so long as it does not violate the rights of others, nor impose on the property of others. There is always an overlap with respect to the law, the prime directives remain life, liberty, and the right to pursue happiness so long as the property of others is respected. In this case it is the secondary property of ideas, of feelings, of the thoughts within self. This amendment drew from the Pilgrims and the Puritans, peoples that came to this country many years ago to leave behind the oppression of beliefs they were exposed to in Europe.

But now we have a big backlash. Now we have special interest groups that are challenging the basic premise of freedom as defined under this constitutional amendment. This is when people feel so strongly about their subject that the balance does not exist, that no dissenting voice can be heard. It is the consequence of a limited democracy, which is a really plausible institution, but one which butts head with extremely strong opinion. It gets into the 51% vs the 49%, and whether simple majority is sufficient to over-ride the rest. This is a very slippery slope, because 49% is almost 50%, and although 10% is nowhere near 50%, it is within definition and intent of protection of rights. Can a formula do the job? I think not, and the reality is that unless people acquiesce and accept the law of land as defined by the numeric, we would not even have a lawful society. So we jump from the statistical to the moral, and again see a slope that is offering both the best and the worst. It really comes down to the threat to each of our own personal way of viewing the world-financially, morally, intellectually, physically.

Dissent is good, it promotes conversation and compromise so long as the parties are consenting adults and not rabid proponents. It really is what our country has tried to promote- free and honest discussion of opposing views.

Democracy is not a fast process. Especially not so for thinking people, of which we have many, but yet some are driven by things other than logical thought process, unfortunately many by what ends up being extreme prejudice. I don't think that occurs through pre-disposition, rather through brain washing and disruptive occasions of experience. It is not an easy thing to steer a clear and unbiased course through life, yet if people abide by agreed-to societal laws that amazingly were formed by citizen-people very little different than themselves, we truly can co-exist. That's what the first amendment is all about, agreeing to agree, and agreeing to disagree.

On the touchy subject of religion, I believe the anchor is "faith". For most (I'll say *almost* all, because I don't know all) there is no concrete proof, simply strong belief. And that is fine, because the human psyche needs that anchor, needs to correlate big happenings as well as small into some coherent overview, one that sinks deep into the core of a person and offers some explanation of things beyond our control. Belief is not the same as religion, religion is the surroundings that puts a system into procedural effect. So believe as you will, and that is either by choice or by absorption, both of which helped create your belief system. In this country, the constitution says "I will leave you alone to believe and practice your own faith", but inherent in that statement is the codicil that you do no harm to anyone else per the laws of this country. That means intellectually or physically; do not impose on the property of others, our laws say the property of <u>others</u> belongs (guess what) to <u>others</u>.

The trouble is that in many instances, and to too many people, beliefs become threatened by interpretations by others, and there is a reactive backlash to threats, real or imagined. Unfortunately as well, some beliefs are extremely aggressive, and although World War 2 overcame a xenophobic view, another has risen in the world, one that has fomented and grown maliciously, and once again there is major threat in the world in the name of unbending fervor. In these United States, this puts its citizens in a terrible quandary wherein the balance between tolerance and unbridled catastrophe is creating extreme polarization, and a wavering of the interpretation in the constitution, one that looks at religious freedom and then looks at safety and protection of life and liberty.

So the test is at hand, resurfaced.

On the touchy subject of discrimination, we find another extreme. The law is clear, there will not be discrimination, but the social mores of society are so deeply imbedded, that the law faces an uphill battle with a large segment. Look at religion, look at personal belief, look at race, look at poverty levels, look at educational levels, even look at customs of different peoples. Well, America is a melting pot, that's the premise, that's the promise, that's the fact. But the implementation, which should be simply acceptance, falls on too many deaf ears. There are ways to try and overcome the shortfall, starting with the law, then logic, then peaceful dissent, and then unfortunately, we get to rabble-rousing and aggressive behavior. To reach through these stages is a process that acts like a bull in a China shop, there is pushing, there is confrontation, and there can be violence.

How to handle this is not an easy pathway, because of the depth of the feelings and emotions. Everything relates to upbringing, what a person believes; but perception is as big a piece as truth, and unfortunately, sometimes the two are the same and the consequences fly out of control. So civil disobedience, outright rioting, and sometimes violent outcomes, are things that happen. But life and property are sacrosanct, and crossing that line violates the highest levels of our agreements within our civilization.

Take the number 1 (one). It is very easy to make that number 2 (two), and so on. All it takes is repetition, and you eventually have a major impact. So when one event occurs, it rapidly duplicates in the wrong environment, and this is the big issue. The biggest offense to life and property is the loss of either.

Now we come to the next phrase of protection within the constitution, that of freedom of speech and of the press. Speech is an easy one- clearly the right to say what one thinks and feels is part

of the concept that the Constitution protects. But once again, with codicils, in this case against incitement to riot and attempts to overthrow the government, which speaks to <u>UN</u>-peaceful assembly. The wonderful part of this process is that through lawful means, it is possible to institute change. The process involves careful considerations and then the dissemination of the effort. So free speech and assembly allow for the spreading of ideas within the constraints of safety and non-threat. And freedom of the press allows for wide-spread dissemination of these ideas, but here we have a conundrum in that bias enters into the equation.
The reporting of news is not the same as commentating on the news. Both are perfectly acceptable, reporter and commentator, but must be separated to the degree that the listener/watcher is aware of the source of the positions espoused. This has become part of our political and social processes. Politics, that unbelievably intertwined perspective, has become deeply enmeshed with the financial welfare of large groups, such as unions, cause-based movements (abortion/anti-abortion), large corporations looking to improve business perspective, religious zealots, environmental groups, "save the snail-darter" groups.

I am thinking of freedom of speech as I watched the Republican primary debates moving towards the 2016 election. The field had 17 potentials and is slowly narrowing down. The debates are really telling a story at this point. Firstly, about bias- the debate hosted by CNN and then by NBC both had aggressively confrontational formats and mediators. So the candidates were really hampered by the constraining and deliberately antagonistically worded subject questions. I took from these debates that the "free press" in terms of certain stations, papers, groups, was really biased and instead of newscasters, they were news commentators carrying over all their prior rhetoric.

AMENDMENT 2   (Guns)

"A well regulated Militia, being necessary to the security of a free State, the right of the people to keep and bear Arms, shall not be infringed."

This has two sides, because although the original intent was to assure the ability to retain the security of a free state, there has been blatant abuse of the right to bear arms, resulting in a large criminal element taking advantage of the amendment's offer. And on top of that, free enterprise in the form of illegal or uncontrolled gun sales has been rampant.

So first, let's look at some possibilities:
- Is this really a "right", I mean a natural one, or is it a societal offering?
- Is this right a universal, in that any and all people (should) have it?
- Or is this right a quasi-universal, in that any and all people "qualified" will have the right?
- Does it apply to all arms- for example concealed and unconcealed, various calibers, automatic, and lastly are arms to be construed as firearms only, or any kind of weapon?
- Does State mean the United States, or the individual states within it- who should be the issuing agency?
- What constraints are imposed, such as selling of ammunition, licensing, open carry?
- Implicit is the necessity of the citizen to secure (and assure) freedom- does this influence charter and domain?
- Does this speak strictly to a government-formed militia, and thus, the right of the people is really for their representative militia to bear arms?

Some of these probably sound like inane questions to many who have thought this through, yet we are currently in quite an internal (within the nation) antagonistic state of affairs, with significant conflict over wording, intent, and implementation.
So firstly, some of the Supreme Court rulings:

1939, "United States v. Miller"-restricting access to shotguns or machine guns by citizens outside the military is permissible.
2008, "DC v. Heller"- cannot ban handguns, it is an individual right; possession of dangerous and unusual weapons is not a right.

All of this gets back to a basic premise of society, which is that if you agree to live within society, you agree to do so in a law-abiding manner or accept the violation's consequences. Unfortunately, interpretation immediately posits potential noncompliance. The idea that if you don't like a law you can go through legal means to change it has a problem when it comes to straight-forward interpretation of the law. It is therefore not clear what is a violation unless the interpretation is recognized as invalid. Note that although the court has recognized a Second Amendment right to bear arms, it has not recognized an absolute right of everybody to bear arms, of all kinds, at all places, in all circumstances. Also note that the second amendment does not clearly prohibit increased limitations on access to guns and therefore by default allows for lawful gun regulation, such as background checks and bans on assault weapons.

The question of jurisdiction, such as "state's rights" vs. national policy, is really easy to answer by recognizing that the Constitution was written as a document of the nation, and the security of a free state must refer to nation, not an individual piece thereof, therefore the umbrella covers the pieces with a national policy.

One of the things that is critical, and that we must always remember, is responsibility. This means that if guns are legal carry, then it is the responsibility of the law-makers to ensure that there will be laws governing ownership, use, illegality. Nothing comes for free. There will be people who want guns for various reasons, and so law must be in place and enforced so that who gets them is clear, who has them is clear, illegality is clear, punishment is clear, and the fact of refusal to issue a license does not in the least insure that the requestor will not get what he/she wants anyway. In any population sample there are always norms and extremes. This is true of any survey, and ones that look at emotional stability and moral intent will show fringes. I have jumped from pure law to morality and its application within the jurisdiction of law. There is no absolute assurance that the checks and balances of the law weed out those whose moral standards assure issues with gun ownership. There is no absolute regarding refusing someone a license that also assures that the individual will not circumvent this refusal. In these cases, the only assurance is punitive, and the threat of such must contain an over-riding assurance that violation will result in legal ramification. Even this is not fool-proof, because there is a very large fringe that operates outside the law. Essentially the rule there is that they are in business to do what they want to do, and capture is the equivalent to bankruptcy of their illegal business. It therefore behooves the system to always find the illegal violators, and that has been the case for all of mankind's existence, whether we talk about theft or any other violation of society's laws.

Bottom line is that we must have as high a level of protection as there is of violation.

AMENDMENT 3   (Military Quartering)

"No soldier shall, in time of peace be quartered in any house, without the consent of the Owner, nor in time of war, but in a manner to be prescribed by law."

This amendment looks within, and speaks mainly to the need to place military personnel into strategic military locations. It clearly implies that in times of peace, military personnel will be housed through military channels, not forcing private citizen acquiescence. It also reins in the concept of universal control and loosely interprets eminent domain by assuring that this can only be done by national law requirement. It says that government has the responsibility to protect citizen rights to life, liberty, and the pursuit of happiness, and that it is government responsibility to insure military power is available to meet these needs.
One might say "this is too far out of the flow of things that I know, and so who cares". However, at the time, military quartering was not too far in the past, and the need to do this was necessary but onerous. Well, so the far-thinking writers looked very far ahead, to possible other turmoil, and the potential that this might be necessary once-again. And now, it would require law to allow it. THE LAW: the thing upon which our country was founded and based, a path to accomplishment, but using democracy to so achieve.

This is so much more than simply armed forces quartering. This broadens to look at anything that government wants to accomplish, and saying that nothing can be done without either consent or due process, in this case both in time of war, or not. Curtailment of government edict is still a reflection of assuring personal freedom. Laws however, can be established using extreme power such as war-time authority, and thus giving our chosen representative government the ability to operate without undue impedance.
But back to military quartering: it all relates to property and property rights. Under ordinary peace-time circumstances, the military has its own quartering, through the use of either government owned housing or privately contracted agreement. When the military is called upon, and not until then, other arrangements

associated with deployment, need to be made. Again, with forethought, military deployment is a planned event, basically a logistic exercise in providing support for the force. For the US, such planning entails careful combination of requirements and sufficient funding to support the planning. So based on this amendment, which is used as the premise for logistical dispersion, the funding must be in place for government supported quartering.

Let's segue into other areas. I would venture that during prior time of war, although quartering was probably done, that the resultant discord of the populace was a noted trend. Quartering opens the door to potential offences and distortions, it places burden on the populace. Rationalizing that citizens support the effort, then the reason for unpopularity would only be behavior.

Of course, although the amendment notes no quartering except in time of war, and by law, we must recognize that martial law might be in effect, or even presidential executive authority, thus by-passing the constraint that seems to have been effected. If martial law is in effect, one must presume that issues have reached a point where normalcy is out the window. On the other hand, executive decree has more latitude, if a popular president has imposed it, then it may be acceptable, however, in the case of issue this may be considered over-reach. This particular amendment has more historical stimulus than would seem appropriate, but maybe not nowadays when unhappiness is in the air.

AMENDMENT 4   (Search Warrants)

"The right of the people to be secure in their persons, houses, papers, and effects, against unreasonable searches and seizures, shall not be violated, and no Warrants shall issue, but upon probable cause, supported by Oath or affirmation, and particularly describing the place to be searched, and the persons or things to be seized."

This is a country of laws, set up to protect the citizenry, so only an agreed-to requirement can violate the privacy of its citizenry. There are no two sides to this story, clearly if there is cause, then there should be capability. This is a necessity to prevent lawlessness. Another office other than the police (who represent the executive branch) must be part of the process to maintain the concept of checks and balances. When we comply with the essence of this law by showing a reasonable requirement, and show it to a third and supposedly impartial party (the judiciary), then so long as impartiality is maintained, this provides a workable solution. Notice that the amendment recognizes the external conditions that allow for search and seizure.

Nowadays, this can be expanded to such things as information technology. Loosely examined, Apple had proudly created a hopefully "non-violate-able" i-phone IOS so that privacy was assured. Then the government wished them to un-create that capability to use the data for criminal prosecution. I believe that privacy is the key word and that currently there is no assurance that over-riding that privacy, even in the hands of government, is a thing that should be foisted on private industry by the heavy hand of a government. If the government can unilaterally act as hackers, that is a different issue, and should fall under this amendment, but not the forcing of private industry to support breaking down proprietary capabilities nor personal privacy.

So what this amendment does is offer a legal path to obtain reasonable search and seizure capability, but only within its charter.

Now we can break this down further beyond the "legal-eeze" of its basis. There are two positions and many considerations to review, those of the search-er and those of the search-ee. Everything moves in an accord until there is some sort of violation, usually by the potential search-ee against some rules of the search-er. Rules of the search-er are usually based on rules of law that have been approved either by the populace through popular vote or by the search-er representing by either election or appointment the very same populace. But spin can happen, and extreme positions can be foisted and search and seizure can be selectively questionable. Here is the place where the judicial branch is required to assure firstly that the authority for the warrant has correctly authorized the warrant, and then if the results are used to identify corresponding law-breaking and chargeable activity, that the judicial branch assures that sufficient executive branch argument suitably makes a case for the action and the consequence.

The other side of the coin is the consideration by the search-ee of such an affront on personal space. Firstly in allowing the warrant to represent law-abiding intrusion, and secondly to assure that consequences of such results are properly framed.

There are therefore checks and balances on both the initiation and the results of a warrant. This does not handle the consequences of placing the warrant and results in the inappropriate or illegal categories, and for that suitable jurisprudence and restitution are available. Restitution would be determined commensurate with the degree of illegality, the other end of the spectrum of the use of the results of the warrant.

We are surely talking about personal property, and the sacrosanct nature there-of, and if and when violation of that covenant is permissible. That is why there needs to be buy-in by the citizen to this specific aspect of societal rights, and why there absolutely needs to be checks and balances to assure no flagrant violations are built into the system. After all, we are a society of people, and people are not 100% pure, neither on the side of lawlessness nor on the side of lawfulness. Scary to recognize that the concept of the state can over-ride the concept of private property.

Words like "unreasonable" are subjective. That fine line has not been defined by this amendment, leaving its definition open to interpretation of the times. This is never good, because it then places onus on the judicial branch to make decisions, and these will be made with the personal bias of the judiciary. As an example, the Supreme Court consists of nine judges, and they are appointees of the president with concurrence of the Congress. How political this gets is a matter of who sits in the various offices. The checks and balances are in effect, but they themselves place a political bent on the solution. No time is more important than that of the 2016 election, wherein the court sits at 4 liberals and 4 conservatives, and the ninth judge awaiting decision time. Could a neutral judge be appointed? You bet, but that would not ring well with the political nature of the two presidential candidates, Trump and Clinton. This very day is election day, and so the choices will fall out. But a good look at the process uncovers significant flaws, all relating to the human element.

AMENDMENT 5 (Rule of and Due Process of Law)

"No person shall be held to answer for a capital, or otherwise infamous crime, unless on a presentment or indictment of a Grand Jury, except in cases arising in the land or naval forces, or in the Militia, when in actual service in time of War or public danger; nor shall any person be subject for the same offence to be twice put in jeopardy of life or limb, nor shall be compelled in any criminal case to be a witness against himself, nor be deprived of life, liberty, or property, without due process of law; nor shall private property be taken for public use without just compensation."

Boy, a mouthful here, and the underpinnings of our democratic society, (although I do have some question about taking private property, even with just compensation- more about that later).   This amendment speaks to criminal justice:
- accusation requires pre-consideration
- if not proven, then it's all over
- cannot force the accused to comply without due process
- consideration required for verdict
- the public cannot commandeer private property without cause and value received

Here is the kernel of the founding of the United States- the removal of arbitrary decisions about property. Property has the expanded definition of meaning your life, your thoughts and ideas, your physical belongings. So a citizen has the confidence that unless performing criminal acts which violate the agreed-to "state" laws, that citizen will receive the full assurance of the government not to interfere in the normal life process, and to assure that if violation occurs then lawfulness will be protected and the violator appropriately chastised.

The under-pinning is that laws have received sufficient review before being enacted so that the agreement of the citizenry is representative.

What I said in chapter 7 regarding misuse of the warrant system applies to the rule of due process. Going beyond warrants for search and seizure, the Grand Jury is a step in the middle of a process between accumulation of fact and accusation of misdeed, and this is taken seriously so that without sufficient cause, citizens will not be placed in status of jeopardy.

The idea that a person need not testify against him/herself really says that corroboration of an event needs to be by outside entities. This does not mean that the person cannot testify if so desired, it is choice and the presumption of innocence protection.

Lately though, it has become in vogue to draw on this very fifth amendment's protection against self-testifying to allow even inquiry to slide down the slippery slope of self-incrimination. Apparently truth is not as important as drawing on the façade of constitutional protection. So the very laws that protect also hide. It does make the burden of proof even harder to achieve, yet the intent is good and thus, the extremes can hide behind it. Oh well, judgement is the result of due process, not the result of gut feel.

In the name of freedom of speech, groups have become vocal with diatribe, and the louder the shouting, the more attention is given by the press and therefore the more attention is paid by the listening public. This sway of public opinion jumps from fact to decibels in short order, and in the hands of seasoned rabble-rousers can quickly hijack what could be called a "cause" and sway the rhetoric towards other ends. In the guise of fairness, the rhetoric is given as much or more time than the facts. The legal process has a timeline associated with it, one that is intended to insure that due process is taken, that facts are accumulated, that a proper scenario is prepared and presented. This is not the case with emotional presentations, they are designed to circumvent the process and produce blind acceptance through transference of conditions into the scenario desired.

Such is the recent and on-going situation with the "Black Lives Matter" group, which jumps on any situation and creates their own scenario to go along with their own goals. Clearly, there is a basis for the thesis, but there is a proper venue for exercising the rights of the protesters. Ignoring facts, over-riding the justice process, immediately jumping over the incident and trampling logic, screaming louder than anyone else- these are tactics.

AMENDMENT 6   (Prosecution)

"In all criminal prosecutions, the accused shall enjoy the right to a speedy and public trial, by an impartial jury of the State and district wherein the crime shall have been committed; which district shall have been previously ascertained by law, and to be informed of the nature and cause of the accusation; to be confronted with the witnesses against him; to have compulsory process for obtaining witnesses in his favor, and to have the assistance of counsel for his defence."

So firstly, when you are accused, it is with the presumption of innocence, that in fact, you are a suspect, no matter what the crime, unless you have confessed, and then the burden is 100% on the state to do all the right things, with the premise that you are NOT GUILTY. Thus, the words imply minimum inconvenience (although that is a relative reference), and with every aspect providing you with the opportunity to support innocence until PROVEN GUILTY. The State looks to allow the local mores, customs, and people of the area to prevail, so that idiosyncrasies can be recognized.

Accusations and justice are paramount to the process, and due process means that persons cannot be simply taken and sequestered, but that there is a defined path that leads to clearing up the situation. That beats the idea of "confinement without recourse", however there is a basic premise that oversight exists to assure that the letter of the law is followed and impropriety does NOT abound.   Steps are built in to force guidelines leading to clear development of the prosecution; and having a clear understanding of the charge, a clear view of the presentations of the witnesses, and the ability to support your own claim and use witnesses, and especially the ability to obtain supporting counsel.

To me, the two most important features this amendment offers to citizens is the ability to clearly understand the problem, and assuring that the accused has necessary supporting guidance through the legal process.

There are many places in the civilized world that do not have such protections in place. Logic works most of the time, but a good and proper entrenched procedure is paramount to protecting the citizen.

There are always some interesting asides. One of these is the competency of both the prosecution and the defense. A prime example is the O.J. Simpson case in which the prosecution completely botched their case in so many ways that the door was completely open for eliminating relevant testimony and material. Just to name a few: the glove, blood-stains on the auto upholstery, contaminated DNA samples, Mark Fuhrman's rants, inability to find the large bag stuffed into the airport trash. And the defense played some of its very best moments not only by making a sham of the evidence, but appealing to a jury through racial bias. It was also a sham that the jury selection process had to be so involved with publicity, that the jury had to be sequestered to such a degree, that the trial was televised, that the judge became inured with self. This case showcased both the pluses and minuses of the law, specifically this amendment. It allowed some extremely minor credibility to the verdict, yet the doubt remains itself extreme to too large a degree.

Law enforcement in the United States has always been plagued by consideration of bias, and in today's environment it is essential that the unbiased observer (the camera, the recorder) becomes a necessary tool to ensure that law enforcement actions do not become subject to bias by the populace. In this case I mean religious perspective, racial perspective, gender perspective. Too many causes jump on the bandwagon and twist and mock the legal system. Unfortunately, too often the door is opened by actual bias on the part of the few, which makes the many take stock and operate on a cautious and fearful level. There is a terrible bias by socialistic leanings that grabs any event to besmear legal attempts at resolution. There is a tendency to assume that he who shouts the loudest wins, and the organized vocal few are definitely the loudest.

AMENDMENT 7   (Jury Trial)

"In Suits at common law, where the value in controversy shall exceed twenty dollars, the right of trial by jury shall be preserved, and no fact tried by a jury shall be otherwise re-examined in any Court of the United States, than according to the rules of the common law."

It must be assured that the deck is never stacked, and that a reasonable view is available. Of course this is not criminal but common law, and this amendment tries to remove bias from any disposition. If you have ever been through the jury selection process, it is obviously tedious and tends in the favor of the defendant, although both the prosecution and the defense have rights to dismiss potential jurors for any or no apparent reason. This amendment relates to common law, not criminal law, however, the jury selection process is similar. The difference is the more stringent requirement of the burden of proof necessary for a conviction in a criminal case.

As set up now, jury duty is a selective responsibility of the citizenry to fulfill. However, it is easy to look at a busy schedule and decide that other things are more important, and thus attempt to circumvent the process- "I am biased, I have very urgent responsibilities", all the rationalized reasons to continue on with your life without this uncomfortable interruption. But, that is not what it is about, rather consider that this particular responsibility tries to insure that the law of the land is not a farce, that citizen awareness of both issues and protections are suitably addressed, and that citizens are involved in the process. Part of the process is the careful examination of potential jurists to cull out the mind-sets that would circumvent the neutrality of the assembled jurists and the attempt at insuring that evidence and not pre-disposition are at the fore.

And finally, it is intended that before the parties are brought to trial, that either the prosecution feels that the evidence is sufficient to provide a verdict, or if a personal matter, then the parties both feel that sufficiency is there to support their respective side to the case. In that light, once brought to trial and a decision reached, the case will not be brought back (unless new and sufficient evidence qualifies it for re-examination).

The subject of jury duty and jury make-up is a complex issue. As discussed, one of the desirables is that a jury member feels a proper responsibility to the assignment. For that purpose, queries by the attorneys, the prosecutors, the judge, are all geared toward deleting bias. However, it is still too easy for a potential jurist to mask true feelings. So is this the best method for jury selection? Is it possible that in fact a separate job classification of "jurist", populated by dedicated persons with penchant for truthfulness, would be a suitable alternative? It was suggested in Ray Bradbury's "Stranger in a Strange Land", and makes a lot of sense although the power given to this class of people would be sought by many who would twist it. But even so, the possibility of manipulating a jury is real and carries heavy fines in recognition of its reality.

The idea of a judge performing the sole decision-making is real in many cases, those cases deemed not requiring a jury for disposition.

Getting back to the jury concept, the judge always must admonish the jury to pay attention to the facts and the judge's instructions, and not to get diverted. But people are people, with emotion, with preconceptions, with bias, even with inability to slot into the requirements established because the questioners miss something. Of course, as I mentioned, part of the system is that no 'vetting process can absolutely assure impartiality. Even without bias, malice, or forethought, mistakes can be made. That is one of the reasons that the death penalty, with its absolute finality if followed to completion, is such a controversial issue. When a criminal gets into the business of lawlessness and criminality, that person accepts that this is a business, and bankruptcy is when you are caught, and the potential penalty is well advertised. The danger is for a wrong decision.

AMENDMENT 8   (Bail)

"Excessive bail shall not be required, nor excessive fines imposed, nor cruel and unusual punishments inflicted."

This gets into value and personal judgment, since the words excessive, cruel, unusual, are totally subjective. However, the concept is correct, in trying to force authority to look carefully at "punishment and fitting the crime". Whether the opportunity for bail will be available is left in disposition to authority and interpretation of the law. But given that the accused is within the legal right to be eligible for bail, then this is an extension of "innocent until proven guilty". It is the essence of American jurisprudence, that you may be charged, and if you are not a flight-risk, and if your charge is not of an extremely dangerous nature, then your word and your bond are sufficient to allow you mobility.

This all relates to how society views its citizens. It is a moral code embedded in a judicial code. One thing it says it that the particular situation is open to eventual proof of guilt or innocence. There is an industry of bail-bond loan businesses who are betting on certain basic requirements, including that the individual will honor his word and his pledge as well as whatever is offered as collateral. That is not to say that this entire premise is clean. If you notice above, there are lots of "howevers" premised in the offer of bail-bond.

The reality is that the idea is a right one (of course it is), one that gives the benefit of the doubt if that is a possibility. The law looks through the eyes of the judge in the decision to allow bail, and that has the supposed fact that the judge has been suitably schooled and inured in the rightness of the law.   The trouble is that the judge and the offer of bail is only one portion of the equation. The bail-bond is the second piece of the puzzle. Is there enough proprietary reality in the bond number to assure that the bail-ee will satisfy the legal requirements? In a way, that is the job of the bondsman, whose money is provided to satisfy the requirement. Is the collateral sufficient for the task or is it put up as a sacrifice only?

Maybe part of the bail-bond needs to be the attachment of GPS-based trackers so that the bail-ee is given titular freedom and the system is given assurance of compliance.

The amendment notes that excessive bond is also out of bounds, but here comes the subjective evaluation of how much that bond should be, and does it in any way relate to the circumstance of the potential bail-ee. Firstly, bail is money, so this places things into a physical property perspective, and the value of is strictly related to what a person perceives. Now for many, there would be no thought of skipping out, and that bail is strictly for the convenience of "controlled freedom".

This system has its flaws but also its positive side, which far outweighs the negative- although there is an overarching principle that if you leave, there are many agencies that would be activated to get the party back under rein.

Look again at the wording of this amendment. It is a protection for the presumption of innocence, bail as a concept is a given. So the law and law-abidingness, the foundation of a free society, are tempered by the get-out-of-jail card. Still, not all accusations carry the codicil of bail as an assuaging element. This is the checks and balances of the system, checking on the balance, so to speak. The bigger issue is that the legal system MUST be infallible, and the punishment MUST fit the crime. The business of criminality is very real, every criminal assesses the probability of bankruptcy, in this case getting caught and sentenced. There must be absolutely no doubt that the criminal will be caught, that the criminal will be convicted, that he will be justly sentenced, and that the sentence will be implemented to completion. This is easy to say, and each element of this chain is critical. Today's modern technology is helping to get the first step completed, whether it is by monitoring apparatus, through some cyber concept, through witnesses, there are more ways in highly civilized countries to insure that violators of the law will be caught. Of course, the presumption of innocent until proven guilty is a stalwart that protects every citizen, and the law industry is set up on the premise that the prosecution absolutely must satisfy the requirements of proof, whether civil or criminal, this forces the legal system to expend phenomenal amounts of time (and thus cost) to meet the burden. But this is where it is critical that each step taken builds the iron clad case. Then there are the plea-bargain issues, where it is simply expedient to accept a lesser effect and thus smooth the moves within the system. This is a hard but tempting path, especially when proof-positive is lacking. Here again, bending a moral view, or compromising a legal view, are always possibilities, but one hopes that this is a few and far-between result which is well within the parameters of the distribution curve.

Case in point was the recent 2016 election cycle regarding charges of forms of illegal , law-breaking activity. Status helped sway the decision process. There was where set and setting went against the legal pathway.

AMENDMENT 9   (Overarching Rights)

"The enumeration in the Constitution of certain rights shall not be construed to deny or disparage others retained by the people."

Other rights means anything not discussed within the Constitution, and that means interpretation is required to assure there are no conflicts, or if there are, that they become well understood, well analyzed, and well dispositioned. This speaks to the two sides of the equation- firstly, that government cannot simply utilize a lawful power to ride rough-shod over its citizenry. Secondly, citizens cannot have tunnel vision and decide that there is a one-sided support system that ignores things not specifically mentioned. Notice that no mention is made of the ability of the states to enact a law against activity of the people, thus allowing control over some of the very rights not discussed in the Constitution.

If you notice, the wording does NOT specifically state whether "other" rights means as noted and written, implied, or not even within purview. So interpretation is clear, that the only clear charter of the Constitution is to follow what it states, not to go out on a limb. There would be a tendency to stretch interpretation per personal preference or even moral leaning, but that is not the intent.

However, once again, the words "others retained by the people" does have the implication that such are already enumerated somewhere, but where?

Oh my gosh, now I see why lawyers and justices are necessary, if only as accumulators of fact and implications. My own personal feeling is that what is not specifically called out is beyond ken, and only because otherwise the umbrella is too broad.

However, let's just bring up States Rights. What about conflict between the federal government's rules and regulations, and those of the various states. Here is where "others" is critical. Here is where the concept of rights retained by the people opens the door to so many forms of interpretation.

Equally important, is the thought that "there oughta be a law", which was a catch phrase of one of the most influential speakers I knew, Mr. Andrew J. Golombos, an astro-physicist turned lecturer who believed in the sanctity of property as being the stalwart and lynchpin of man's inter-relationship with man. What that means is that the tongue in cheek statement really was aiming at how man puts rules all over the place, over everything, and pushes requirement rather that consent.

Are laws always limiting? Or can they give things as well? We know the answer is that laws are firstly to protect, and you can always find a protection that gives something as a consequence rather than as a limit. But if not enumerated somewhere, is any thing a right? Again, the compass must turn inward somewhat, and a guideline would be that if it imposes on the property of someone else without their consent, then it should not be an open invitation to pursue. That is where the government, the law, the thinking, the morals, all need to pass the test of the universal can opener -"whose property is it?" This may in fact be a catchup to pass a law that protects the property of a citizen, but perfection is an asymptotic goal.

So the Declaration and the Constitution both are firm statements of both rule and intent, and this amendment is the front and back door to living under these documents. It opens the door to recognition of the fact that unless the law is written, there is no authority for enforcement of a concept, at least, not at the constitutional level. Then it says go seek out other authority, and unless you find applicability, then there is no actual legal control. Not to say that moral and ethical codes don't play a part, but they are outside the legality of the law.

AMENDMENT 10   (Powers beyond the Constitution)

"The powers not delegated to the United States by the Constitution, nor prohibited by it to the States, are reserved to the States respectively, or to the people."

Oh yes, give me state's rights every time. This takes law and personalizes it by putting authority into more local hands. Who better to know what is necessary in the way of overarching control than the very people who have and are exercising their own mores and standards. By the way, this translates directly to the concept of the electoral college, whereby large local areas are essentially grouped as one on the premise of similarities, however the size of the group still provides only proportional influence as well through the number of electoral seats provided to the states.

There can obviously be concern about conflict between federal and state authority when they both speak to the same subject, such as good old marijuana legality or the death penalty as prime examples. Where charter is identical, then there will be conflict, and here the litmus test is the statement of this 10th amendment. If the Constitution doesn't address it, either directly or obliquely, then the federal government needs to step away. Now if an amendment to the amendment develops, that is another story.

The bottom line on this one is that anything not country or state is in the hands of the people. In California, no better example than the ballot initiative; although its purpose is to create another requirement having been established by the people, but now out of their hands and then placed into the hands of the state. Funny isn't it- that the power of the people could result in giving up that power?

This also goes back to the previous section (amendment 9) which discusses powers not enumerated. Here in amendment 10 is just the slightest bit of ambiguity, because it implies that there are such powers hanging around, and whatever they may be, let's let the states and the people fight it out for who has authority and control. Are these powers even enumerated somewhere? Are they about any specific genre, such as legal or moral or political or financial, or is this amendment simply broad-brushing things and sweeping them into one big collection?

Next step is to determine that if someone claims the power (ie... state or people) how does it get recognized as now a controllable commodity, what method defines ownership, how does it get controlled?

This amendment is an adjunct to amendment 9, which says the constitution does not address anything more than what is contained within it. Implication is that if you don't like something, move out or make lots of noise, because you have the ability to give voice to your standards and with sufficient support you get your way. This means that you can help get something either done or overturned if you feel strongly enough, all you need is sufficient like-minded citizens.

SELECTED OTHER AMENDMENTS

AMENDMENT 13 *"SECTION 1- Neither slavery nor involuntary servitude, except as a punishment for crime whereof the party shall have been duly convicted, shall exist within the United States, or any place subject to their jurisdiction.*
SECTION 2- Congress shall have power to enforce this article by appropriate legislation."

Pretty straightforward, each man is free so long as the contract between state, society, and citizen is not violated, with a definite legal and lawful verification of that fact. Then there is the possibility, if the legal system so deems, that the form of punishment shall fit the crime, and be bounded by the constitutional and jurisprudent limits. In the case of such conviction, involuntary servitude is the form of punishment. Using Webster as a reference, the term slavery has three meanings: 1- submission to a dominating influence, 2- the practice of slaveholding (a person held in servitude as the chattel of another). 3-the state of a person who is chattel of another. Involuntary servitude is in fact the usage, while definition 2 of slavery would be the only relative reference, although the concept of chattel (person held as personnel property) is just not part of the judicial sentencing within our society of the United States of America. So in terms of sentencing, once convicted, the party is put under the control of the incarceration system.
It seems to me, that sentencing after conviction means that there was violation of published law and its verification through the legal system, and that the range of punishment is well understood, and that the party has therefore placed him/her-self in the position of requiring judgement for offense committed. Here is the clear path of action and consequence, and the law is there to provide a hindrance to offending, but is also there as the consequence.

Throughout our normal societal interactions and mores, there is criminal offence in the violation discussed and covered in the 13th amendment, and that is the power of the 13th amendment. No one forces a party to do things they do not wish to do, except as one places oneself in such a position, thus the validity of punishment for offense duly convicted. Society offers freedom, with very few constraints except that another's property belongs to them, not to someone desiring it, and that a contract must be the source of exchange, or else the law will be invoked. This is the power of the 13th amendment; that a person must both violate the law and be convicted of so doing, in order to fall under the punishment system.

 Section 2 is interesting as well. It puts teeth to this amendment, it says that the government of the United States, and not the states themselves, is empowered to assure compliance with this requirement, independent of local or state law. As with many others, this amendment is obviously held in the highest esteem and gets the authority and backing it has based on a moral perspective as well as social, political, and criminal ones.

AMENDMENT 14 "*SECTION 1- All persons born or naturalized in the United States and subject to the jurisdiction thereof, are citizens of the United States and of the State wherein they reside. No State shall make or enforce any law which shall abridge the privileges or immunities of citizens of the United States; nor shall any State deprive any person of life, liberty, or property, without due process of law; nor deny to the person within its jurisdiction the equal protection of the laws.*"

Let me start out by saying that the founding fathers wanted to offer the blessings of this country to all people, and built in a definition that gave citizenship through sweeping purview. Being born in the United States is used as the criteria for all rights, and being naturalized is raised to as high a standard as birth here. No discussion ensues about how a person got here, thus begging the question of illegality of the initiation of the process, thus premising legality. Note, premising legality, thus premising law-abiding constituents. This comes under challenge by appeal to kindness, goodness, other –nesses, it comes under challenge by forces that would over-ride the premises of this country.
One of the first physical things that define a country is its borders and boundaries. Those become nationally and internationally

inviolate, yet porosity to some degree has forever existed based on violation of the premise of law-biding citizenry. At this time, there are extremely deep feelings and tempers relating to alien persons within the borders of the country. Alien is not POLITICALLY CORRECT at this time, rather "undocumented individuals" is the term that some would use. No difference, because the term alien, according to Webster, simply means "a foreign-born resident who has not been naturalized and is still a subject or citizen of a foreign country". Oh my goodness, isn't that awful, to call a real person by their status? Well, there are real solutions, not PC solutions, that should in fact be enacted.

Firstly, take a look at the laws. I see two diametrically opposed paths- one is to change this amendment and revise the definition of citizenship availability to exclude those persons born from illegally entered persons. The second way would be to clearly include such "statused" children within the purview of this amendment. Either way is using the law to define the law, and that is the right way to pursue resolution; public demonstration is perfectly acceptable because it is protected by freedom of speech and it gets out a strong message by the vocal few.

There needs to be a look at the morality of this amendment as well. If it never existed, then illegal would be illegal, and birth would not be surfaced to acknowledgment. No rights would be forthcoming, no status would be granted except illegal. But the amendment exists, and in a country governed by law, it clearly states that citizenry is a given. So now look at two categories: grandfathering offers that if you satisfy the requirements, then you are golden. However, if the amendment was changed and dropped the citizenry, it would only apply to the future as of the time of approval, retroactivity for the new wording should never be a codicil.

Sections 2-5 not discussed

AMENDMENT 15 *"SECTION 1- The right of citizens of the United States to vote shall not be denied or abridged by the United*

States of America by any State on account of race, color, or previous condition of servitude."

Note the word "citizens". This does not mean tenant, it does not mean migrant, it clearly specifies the larger and all-encompassing term that means if you are not a citizen and I mean a legal citizen, then voting is not available. Interest in issues is certainly acceptable, and lobbying for issues is acceptable, but when it comes right down to it, if you do not fall under the umbrella of citizen as defined by the Constitution, as made available through this great country of ours, then it is the non-citizens responsibility to apply through legal means to enter that compact, or to legally lobby as loudly as they wish, but the vote is not available. Now here we also jump into not only the nation, but the individual states as well. It also must flow down to county, to city, to hamlet, to unincorporated area.

This section is focused on assuring such rights to citizens no matter ethnicity or prior conditions regarding freedom.

I note how extremely important the right to vote really is, when I examine the most recent election of 2016, in which four parties and two main candidates offered themselves to the populace. This election offered the very worst of alternatives, in that based on the past 20 or so years, the platforms of the parties have become extremely polarized, and the candidates themselves have become extremely polarized. On the Democratic Party side, there was an unexpected outpouring for a socialist candidate which forced the favorite to adapt directions not intended. Hillary Clinton had an extremely blemished past in her involvement with her "Clinton Foundation", with decisions made on Benghazi, with disastrous decisions on using her own private server to mix personal, private, government, classified material- thus violating federal law on both a personal and classified level. Add to that a rather grating personality. On the plus side, she had gender, experience, finances, and platform appeal to a large segment of the population.

Donald Trump came along as the quasi-Republican, actually a businessman outsider, and ran a thoroughly grating campaign wherein he showed complete lack of political knowledge, actual decisions to NOT disclose any platform direction, a bull-in-the-china-shop presentation.

And the voters needed to sift through all the chaff, and decide which unpopular candidate was the potentially least damaging to their needs. Here is where the electorate would have to shine, here is where knowledgeable voting acumen would be required, and yet that was not the case. Instead, once again, the voter looked deep within and selected what would best benefit that voter. Now this is not in any way wrong, because after all, we the populace are made up of individuals. Policy and platform must be translated into what each of us gets out of it, and time-horizon is one of the many perspectives that are necessary to such decisions. So voting is extremely important, because what you say is a part of the decision.

Notice that I mentioned four parties, but discussed only two candidates. The other two parties and their candidates never got into the mix, they did not have the financing, the organizations, the acumen. Their message never made it mainstream, and so by default, these candidates were token to our political system. But what an interesting situation would have commenced if either surfaced as viable, then the voting profile would have been completely different, the campaigns of all candidates completely revamped.

We also have an interesting conceptual procedure within the voting system- the Electoral College. This institution was established to offer a voice to each and every area of the country. Representation is defined by the sum of Congressional plus Senatorial seats of a state. This therefore does look at area interests as well as population. In many areas, the plurality defines that all votes go to the highest stakeholder; in some it apportions proportionate to the state's internal voting. (In my opinion, the voting should be proportionate to the ballots cast in the specific politically defined area (in other words, the state), thus providing an area and populace output). At the conclusion, then the final national selection for the office would be based on a representative vote that looks at both local interests (the state) and population proportion (the country). However, this would also tend it toward the popular vote, which does represent the people but not the area. Today, the Electoral Vote selects the winner, and the popular vote merely offers whether a mandate was established or not.

Voting, interestingly enough, has become a major issue during the 2016 election. Apparently, the losing side has decided that they don't like the results (what's new!). But in the past, those who lost were upset but not to an extreme of this nature wherein some are saying "not my president", others are saying "secede", others are screaming to call out the militia, and fringes are advocating violence. Read the constitution, read what is above, everyone got their fair and equal opportunity to select, and if it didn't work out to their satisfaction, bear it and support the country, and next time, do more and do better. That is the American Way, not the cry-baby way, not the sore loser way. Oh my goodness, our nation needs a simonize to bring it back into its shiniest of states.

    SECTION 2- The Congress shall have power to enforce this article by appropriate legislation."

Somewhat far-reaching, in recognizing that hot button issues do not just go away with decree. This section gives the executive branch and the judicial branch the charter to insure that this subject become operative.

AMENDMENT 16   *"The Congress shall have power to lay and collect taxes on incomes, from whatever source derived, without apportionment among the several States, and without regard to any census or enumeration."*

Oh woe, here we go. Once the income tax never existed, then it started at ½ of 1%, and look at me now! No question that the government needs to be funded, and no question income tax is one way of obtaining that funding. Well, so is value-added tax or sales tax, and certainly all the various fees abounding. What seems out of sorts is firstly the disproportion of percentages on incomes, the many deductions favored or accepted by the government, and worst, the flagrant non-concern with where the money goes in terms of waste and in terms of the very basic question of "does this funding requirement meet the minimum definition of government charter?" This last is extremely important as noted in prior sections, because taxation and fees are open loops, the source of money required sometimes does not reflect the validity of the requirement. This question MUST be continuously asked, and asked many times on each item to be sure that the answer continues to be a resounding yes. I stress the term minimum definition because of requirements creep, the downfall of many projects. The United States of America is as much a project in functioning democracy as any other project in terms of its own goals. Look at a project and see that the parameters of Cost, Performance, Schedule, Supportability, and Risk are always the factors that must be satisfied, and each requires the support of the management in terms of dedication to the basics of these parameters as criteria for success.

I'd like to segue a bit, and go from taxes into both tariffs and tax breaks. In a previous book, "All Things Relate", I suggested that one method of bringing manufacturing work back into this country was to consider levying tariffs on products produced overseas. I was focusing on a graduated plan of imposing such tariffs aimed at forms of competition that I felt was specifically due to cost and standards of living abroad that placed labor at an advantage out of the US, and therefore created a disaster to competing in-country industry. I felt that graduated tariff which related to reductions with time would offer US industry time to develop suitable competing capability and then the tariff would dissolve. I had focused on tariff because that opened the door to outside country manufacturing costs to be adjusted by the country of manufacturing origin, so that the double sword of internal and external modification was available. My logic was diametrically opposed to my personal beliefs, I feel that the lowest cost for a competitive product produces affluence for the consumer, thus the idea of tariff which is a non-productive form, is the antithesis of my innate beliefs. My logic was that transition is critical to any plan, and the plan to get the US economy into maximum achievement mode is many-pronged and must include job creation within the country.

Well, in addition, I hadn't mentioned another really positive way of accomplishing that goal, and that is tax incentive to produce here and get benefit of cost reduction by bringing jobs back. Again, necessary to have a plan to wean off the dole, and that must be presented and followed as a necessity.

So here we have an amendment that not only finances the government, but even offers methodology for economic advancement. Maybe it was not specifically entertained at the time of the amendment, but surely an interesting government tool. Here we invoke the Declaration of Independence and fold into protection of rights to life, liberty, and the pursuit of happiness. However, there is a real negative impact of taxation and fee-government uses these as the only source of funding, but they are open-looped, if more funding is needed, there is no problem in raising either taxes or fees, there is seldom issue with transferring from other sources of funding, in other words, no incentive to control costs.

AMENDMENT 19   *"The right of citizens of the United States to vote shall not be denied or abridged by the United States or by any State on account of sex."*

A continuation of the 15th amendment by recognizing that they were not inclusive in getting all citizens covered by decree. The political climate goes through time-worn upheaval as the mind-set opens the door to further considerations. But note that it takes a real process to make things happen, that is the beauty of a lawful country, that when a thing is right, then the legal aspect will cover it.
Interesting also that you can see history unfolding, because only at this time had the issue of sex reached a tipping point. Notice that voting had been discussed (amendment 15) relative to race, color, previous servitude, but it took many years of social discourse to develop an inclusive position on sex.

AMENDMENT 26   *"SECTION 1- The right of citizens of the United States, who are eighteen years of age or older, to vote shall not be denied or abridged by the Unite States of by any State on account of age."*

Here we go again. Amendments 15 and 19 started something, and this one continues it. Of course, recognition that there is a different between an informed populace and a mature one, this is the attempt to say that here is an age in which the two come together. Frankly, that is not in the least obvious, because there really is no age that assure either or both, and so here is an arbitrary definition of eligibility that actually ignores the qualifications to cast a meaningful ballot.

"SECTION 2- The Congress shall have power to enforce this article by appropriate legislation."

And again, teeth to the words.

THIS IS BACKROAD COUNTRY- institutions in Agoura, Ca.

AN ASPECT OF THE DECLARATION OF INDEPENDENCE

On the chance that I may sound redundant, and although I've talked about the Constitution, in fact, the preamble to the Declaration contains some of the most powerful thoughts that can exist for a society-**and amongst these are that our government was created to protect citizens' rights to life, liberty, and the pursuit of happiness. That is all our government has been given as charter, and that is more than enough.** I have said this throughout this text, but I don't believe that it can be over-stressed. My reasoning is that we are running rampant with the idea of doing for others, and although there is some moral prerogative to this point of view, that is not a given of society. This is more about freedom to do whatever you want for yourself, and to do for others but only with both your consent and theirs.

On a positive vein, this means that if you are a citizen of the United States, the full authority of the entire country is focused on assuring you these rights. On an even more positive vein, this means that government can create ancillary functionality to satisfy this charter, but not one step beyond. License is not given to simply be a "good guy", rather there is really a specific reading to the golden rule- "do not unto others as ye would not do unto yourself". Notice that the implication is to leave me alone, I can fend for myself, that is what freedom is about, and don't presume to know what a stranger would want for me, because it is my choice, not theirs. I feel very strongly about this, because it is easy to rationalize and slip into the mode of "doing good". As a rather poignant example, let's simply take a stroll into the neighborhood and ask the question if some neighbor would mind if something happened that did not affect them. If the answer is they wouldn't mind, then carry it out of the neighborhood into the section of town, then the town, then the county, then the state, and finally reach a country level. If in each questioning, many others do not mind because they either don't care or it doesn't affect them, we are on the way to a national law that may have passed due to either lack of interest or by majority, but not unanimously. Unanimous is an extreme, but depending on the rules, 51% may be enough; also note that even 66.7% still leaves 33.3% unhappy with the results.

I put the Declaration's statements under the umbrella of "respect of property", no surprise if you have read any of my earlier text.

That's the nutshell, all the rest is pomp and circumstance.

GRAND FINALE

I have said a fair share, but something is still nagging at me. I know that what I have presented is my gut-feelings, not a legal treatise, and so I am looking at how much more gut there is to feel. Actually, there is plenty; and although some of it may be repetitious to the previous text, it is so important on a human and global level, that at the risk of redundancy, I am going ahead with a diatribe.

For shame firstly, on people who see only the trees and miss the forest. Look ahead and see that the universe is a big place, and that humankind's destiny is entwined with seeing the big picture. Because the small picture will put us out of the running, we will destroy ourselves and all life on the planet. I am thinking about how the United States of America represents only one alternative life style and it focuses on individual man and his destiny, his control of his own life, liberty, and pursuit of happiness. That is what the country had as its originating basis, and that is what was built as a societal premise. And our Constitution is a codex that offers the opportunity to abide. Looking at all the various issues that plague our country, both internal and external, they all come down to respect for property, which is defined as our lives, our word, our intellectual acumen, what we own, our liberty. It's all about respect folks, and the idea that violation of our property is theft. That goes for the burglar, the terrorist, the killer, the adulterer, the liar.... no end to the offenses people impose on one another, and it needs to be said that there is no such thing as a SMALL interference with property- it's all the same, it is violation of respect and acknowledgement, and must be treated as such.
Education is a key. Knowledge is important, but until it is fully absorbed and appreciated and used in practice, it is just book-learning. And because life is all about transition from one level to any another, the concept of de-education is also critical. When your entire moral code is pre-established by earlier events, then simple exposure to something new is insufficient to redirect to a desired new path. Significant effort is required to undo preconceived and acquired viewpoints, emotions, mind-sets.

So here sits our Constitution, the guidance and law for our society, and it is a rock. But it must be appreciated, acknowledged, respected, and accepted for what it is, the guide of a lawful society. Those who wish to change it must do so through the legal channels it offers, those that wish to flaunt it do so at the considerable risk that violation will result in punitive response. Most of all, it is the blueprint that, combined with respect for property, will allow the flourishing of our freedoms and our great country.

Be proud of who you are, what you are, where you are, and where you are going. These were your choices, and upward is a direction of life's arrow, follow through.